Pathway of Dreams

Also by David Proctor

The Quotable Vampire

My Oregon Life: The Memories of a 20th Century Pioneer
(with Elvine Gienger)

Brothers Alpha (A novel)

Pathway of Dreams

Building the Boise Greenbelt

David Proctor

Ridenbaugh Press

Carlton, Oregon

For more information, contact Ridenbaugh Press, P.O. Box 834, Carlton OR 97111.
Printed and bound in the United States of America.
First edition May 2016
10 9 8 7 6 5 4 3 2 1

Library of Congress Cataloging in Publication Data

David Proctor

A Pathway Of Dreams: Building the Boise Greenbelt

Bibliography

1. Boise, Idaho - description. 2. Boise, Idaho - history.

I. Proctor, David. II. Title.

ISBN 978-0-945648-34-5 (softbound)

Cover photographs by David Proctor.

Ridenbaugh Press
P.O. Box 834, Carlton OR 97111
Phone (503) 852-0010
www.ridenbaugh.com
stapilus@ridenbaugh.com

For my mother,

Joan Proctor

Table of Contents

Foreword

by Boise Mayor David Bieter

L ooking back on it now, I think there's a good case to be made that the Greenbelt saved Boise.

Saved our river from over-development and degradation, certainly. But also saved our city as a whole – from mediocrity and regret.

To understand why, we need to look back at the Boise River as it was in the mid-20th century, before the Greenbelt, before the Clean Water Act, and before the widespread realization that a healthy environment and abundant recreation opportunities could be the cornerstones of a livable, prosperous community.

Of course, the Boise River had always been important to the city and to the entire valley. As every Boise grade-schooler knows, the lush stands of willows and cottonwoods lining the river's banks, such a welcome sight to the desert-weary French trappers who came upon them in the early 1800s, are what gave this place its name.

In the century that followed, dams tamed the river's flood-prone fury; canals made the arid valley bloom. The town that Clarence Darrow would describe as "a bright green gem in a setting of blue" was made that way by the revitalizing snowmelt that coursed down from the Rocky Mountain foothills each spring. But by the early 1900s, the Boise River seemed destined to follow the fate of so many of the world's urban streams: as a dead, ugly open sewer, where the effluent and detritus of modern industry was discharged without much consideration of the consequences.

As David Proctor details in this outstanding history of the Greenbelt, the Boise River was for decades viewed mostly as a convenient waste-disposal system or as a barrier (not entirely unwelcome) between the northern and southern parts of the city.

Still, the river was beloved by many. I'm convinced that I am a native Boisean largely due to the river: My Dad used to say, only a bit tongue-in-cheek, that when it came time for him and his new wife to settle down and start a family, my mother explained it very simply to him. "We can live anywhere in the country," she said, "as long as you can see the Boise River from there."

By the 1960s and 1970s, the Boise River was defining but not yet iconic. It took some visionary leaders, some fortunate circumstances, and a whole lot of hard work to create the 25-mile-long park that today protects the Boise River's banks from development while making it accessible to tens of thousands of residents and visitors alike – walkers, runners, and cyclists, who descend on the Greenbelt in all but the most inclement weather. Ours is now one of the cleanest urban rivers in the nation, a popular fly-fishing stream literally steps away from downtown as well as the most heavily used recreational river in the state, thanks to our popular summer float season.

The Boise River, along with our Foothills and its extensive trail system, the Bogus Basin ski area, and countless other outdoor activities within a short drive, have made Boise a mecca for people who want a healthy, inspiring place to do business and raise a family. That, in turn, has helped our city to prosper even in difficult times. It has helped us to avoid some of the difficulties that other American cities have faced as they attempt to compete in the new global economy. It has spared us from the regret of not having preserved and enhanced the very qualities that attracted people to this wonderful place decades and centuries ago.

The important thing, we've learned, is to create a livable city. From that, good things flow, like a life-giving spring runoff.

And we owe it all to the Greenbelt, and to the many minds and hands that built it. David Proctor is here to tell the story. It is a great one, befitting a great city, and the many of us who love it.

For years now I've been traveling to Boise and enjoying your city more than any other I travel to during the year.

The Greenbelt area along the river has been especially enjoyable. Each morning at sunrise I run along the river. The feeling of calm is wonderful. The smells, the animals in a natural setting, the camaraderie with others exercising are very special. I've enjoyed your city and look forward to returning four times next year for both business and pleasure.

It's time I said, "Thank you, Boise, your city is like no other."

Keith Cox
Former men's and women's tennis coach, Weber State College, Ogden, Utah[1]

---

1   Keith Cox, Letters to the Editor, *The Idaho Statesman*, June 15, 1987.

Introduction

"It's a pretty amazing story."

– Wayne Gibbs[2]

It is impossible to overestimate what the ceremony that took place July 22, 1975, meant to the city of Boise. It was a beautiful, sky-blue summer day as the crowd gathered on the banks of the Boise River near 13th Street. There, where the W.E. Clements & Sons Concrete Co., once stood, Idaho Governor Cecil Andrus, Boise Mayor Dick Eardley and Greenbelt Committee chair Ken Pursley dedicated Shoreline Park. It was the first official section of the Boise River Greenbelt. Attended by an audience of city officials, Greenbelt volunteers, shirtless boys, men and women in their best leisure suits and summer dresses, and construction workers in hard hats and jeans, the ceremony marked no less than the spiritual rebirth of a city.

Today, the phrase "quality of life" has become synonymous with the name Boise. That was not yet the case in 1975, and certainly not in the early 1960s when the idea of a linear park along the river was first spoken out loud.

Historically, the stretch of the Boise River that runs through the city, especially where it passes near the city zoo, and another stretch downstream below Ann Morrison Park had been little more than a

---

2 H. Wayne Gibbs, former director of Boise Community Planning and Development, interview with the author, Dec. 12, 2000

running garbage dump. Downstream further, slaughterhouses, factories and individual homes used the river as a convenient disposal service. Rusting car bodies and spikes of rebar scattered along its length helped make the river little more than a long water hazard. Along much of its length, the banks were choked with weeds, vicious thorns and refuse that had not quite made it into the water. It was an inconvenient ribbon of geology the city had to build bridges over. Architecturally, emotionally and financially, the people of Boise had turned their backs on their river.

Boiseans had also turned their backs on downtown. By the 1970s, the businesses and government of Idaho's capital city were in as much trouble as the river. Native son novelist and journalist L.J. Davis' 1974 article "Tearing Down Boise" in *Harpers Magazine* described his hometown, population 75,000, as fatally ill from "an overdose of a fatal witches' brew composed of automobiles, greed, bad planning, good intentions, idiotic architecture, and civic pride." Downtown Boise, he wrote, "gives the impression that it has recently been visited by an exceedingly tidy bombing raid conducted by planes that cleaned up after themselves."

Downtown was deserted, Davis said, the suburbs were sprawling to the west and the Boise Redevelopment Agency was betting its life, and the life of the city, on the construction of an 800,000-square-foot downtown shopping mall that officials estimated would cost between $70 million and $200 million. But the mall was stalled and had been for years while the city and Boise Redevelopment Agency attempted in vain to woo three major department stores to serve as anchors.

"If things go as they are," Davis concluded, "Boise stands an excellent chance of becoming the first American city to have deliberately eradicated itself."[3]

---

3 L.J. Davis, "Tearing Down Boise," *Harper's Magazine*, November 1974.

Rusting car bodies and other debris. Undated but probably from the early 1970s. (courtesy/Gordon Bowen Collection, Boise City Department of Arts & History)

Psychologically, the city also suffered from the aftermath of the Boys of Boise. That scandal, which broke in 1955, resulted in *Time* magazine describing a "homosexual underworld" that had allegedly operated for years in Boise. As the *Idaho Statesman* fanned the panic that followed, dozens of men were arrested, including some highly placed members of the community. The inconsistent prison sentences that resulted ranged from probation to life. The city had barely recovered from that self-righteous, politically motivated witch hunt when, in 1966, author John Gerassi's book *The Boys of Boise: Furor, Vice and Folly in an American City* brought it all back up.[4]

Boise needed a miracle. And it got one, though not one most people would have predicted. It was not a downtown mall, but a greenbelt – a system of parks and connecting public land along both sides of the river that ran through the city. And Boise got it because a handful of founding fathers and mothers stepped forward and volunteered to invest the only capital they had – time, vision, courage and the talent to persuade – to create something that would last for generations.

It was a quintessentially American undertaking: a willingness to venture into the unknown because it was the right thing to do, even though it offered these few pioneers no financial gain, and there was no guarantee their efforts would amount to anything. They looked at a dirty, ignored river and saw what it could be. This was not a government project. The people led. The government and commercial interests followed.

As Greenbelt pioneer Alice Dieter put it, "You have no idea what it took in terms of civic pride all along to do it."[5]

Within a remarkably short time, that civic pride took hold. At first, the general population of Boise embraced the Greenbelt concept warmly, then began to see it as an inherent right. "What had been dreamed of by a few in the '60s became the demand of many in the '80s," said former Parks Director Jack Cooper.[6]

Boise now has 170 acres and 27 miles of linear park and 30 miles of bike paths that pass through 12 developed and three undeveloped parks. The 15 parks total 649 acres of public land.[7]

---

4 John Gerassi, *The Boys of Boise: Furor, Vice and Folly in an American City*, University of Washington Press, 2001.

5 Alice Dieter interview with Troy Reeves, in Boise, July 28, 1998.

6 Jack Cooper, "Boise Greenbelt Capital Projects of the '80s," unpublished written comments, p.1, April 9, 2001.

7 E-mail from Boise Parks and Recreation Department.

Unincorporated Ada County, Garden City and Eagle have followed Boise's example and built their own Greenbelt paths. With these additions, the Greenbelt now measures 21 miles end to end and comprises 57 miles of trail on both sides of the river, including all access roads and divided paths.

The integrity of the riparian zones and vegetation has been restored. The city and volunteers have installed distance markers. Fun runs and all manner of events public and private take place on the Greenbelt and its adjoining parks. The trail itself has become a nearly natural element of the river. The financial benefits to the city are almost beyond counting.

The concept worked so well it proved contagious. Other groups, both in and out of government, are working to extend the path from the Boise city limits through the rest of Ada County, through neighboring Canyon County and further west to the Snake River. If completed, the trail would extend a total of 63 miles.

And within its own boundaries, Boise City has created the Ridge to Rivers plan to establish pathways that will link the river with the public land and more than 130 miles of trails in the Foothills that define Boise's northern border. In 2005, a bike path connected Barber Park, the Greenbelt, the Ridge to Rivers trail system and the Surprise Valley area.[8]

For all this we have a small group to thank – the prescient pioneers who gave birth to the original idea and the relatively small number of Greenbelt Committee members and city officials who have nurtured it for more than 40 years. It is a group of volunteers and professionals who, almost to the person, say their work on the Greenbelt was one of the high points of their lives.

The restoration ethic spread throughout the city.

Today, both the city and the river of Boise are thriving. Downtown was rebuilt without the mall, and has become an anchor for commerce

---

8 Cynthia Sewell, "Southeast Boise to get half-mile bike path," *The Idaho Statesman*, Sept. 12, 2005.

and employment. In addition to its four-season recreational
opportunities, Boise is the home of Albertsons, J.R. Simplot Co.,
WinCo and Micron Technology. Hewlett-Packard has a large presence
here, and other high-tech businesses have become an important part of
the economy.

The river and the Greenbelt have seen corporate and residential
developments spring up along their borders. Wildlife thrives in many
locations. The pathway is used year-round for biking and walking, and
people from throughout Southwest Idaho flock there during the
summer to enjoy the water and shade. Some 125,000 of them[9] float
the six-mile stretch of river from Barber to Ann Morrison parks in
inner tubes and rafts every year.[10] From 1990 to 2003, Ann Morrison
and Julia Davis parks were home to the Boise River Festival, which,
at its peak, drew a million people over its four-day run.[11] Both parks
still play host to a variety of festivals and other events all summer.

Attached loosely to the Greenbelt and Julia Davis Park, the
thriving Boise Cultural District bisected by Capitol Boulevard
supports the Boise Public Library!, the Boise Art Museum, the Idaho
Historical Society State Museum, the Idaho Black History Museum,
the Idaho Ann Frank Human Rights Memorial and The Cabin literary
center.

But in ways more spiritual than purely financial this robust civic
and cultural health can be traced to that summer day at Shoreline Park
on the banks of the Boise River where a brilliant idea from more than
a decade earlier became reality. It was the day Boise's latter-day
quality of life was born. Consider: When relatives or friends come to
visit, where do we take them?

"It gives the city its personality," is the way Elizabeth Van
Zonneveld defined the Greenbelt. "Boise is not just a little desert

---

9 Scott Koberg, director of Ada County Parks and Waterways, author interview, April 16,
2015.

10 *Greenbelt Handbook.*

11 Boise River Festival statistics, August 2000.

city," said Van Zonneveld, who as Betty Kelley was an early Greenbelt coordinator. "It's a lovely, lovely city with an identity, a personality, not due to high-rise buildings or the skyline, but to the personal-use kind of amenities that Boise has. It's a reachable, outdoors, delightful kind of place. It wouldn't be that without the Greenbelt."[12]

---

12 Elizabeth Van Zonneveld, telephone interview with Troy Reeves, from Ocala, Fla., July 27, 1998.

1 The River, the Dams and the Parks

The Boise is one of the "most nearly perfect flood-controlled rivers in the country."

– US Army Corps of Engineers

Before the Greenbelt, before the parks, before the dams, before the city, there was the river. What today's residents know as the Boise River results from the joint efforts of four tributaries: The North Fork and the South Fork of the Boise, both of which empty into the Middle Fork of the Boise, plus Mores Creek, which joins up after a trip through Idaho City. All four flow out of the mountains north and east of the city, then join forces to run about 60 miles through Boise, Garden City, Eagle, Caldwell, Notus and Parma. The river eventually enlists with the Snake River as it moves north to join the Columbia.

During the 1700s and 1800s, if not before, the Shoshoni, Paiute, Bannock and Nez Perce gathered near where the Idaho Highway 21 extension now runs east of the city. The area was called "cop-cop-he-pash," or "much cottonwood" or "meeting place."[13] When French traders came into the area in 1774, they found a Native American village located at the hot springs east of Table Rock that was later

---

13 *The Idaho Statesman*, The Greenbelt: A Treasure Valley Labor of Love (special section), "A Greenbelt Chronology," September 28, 1999.

developed into an exclusive club known as Kelly Hot Springs.[14] By 1811, abundant wildlife made the area a popular and lucrative trapping ground for fur companies. The French-Canadian trappers began to refer to the river valley, perhaps struck by its contrast with the surrounding desert, as "Boissie," or "wooded." Washington Irving, who never set foot in Idaho, popularized the name when he used it in his book *The Adventures of Captain Bonneville*,[15] in which he described the area this way: "The country about the Boise or Woody River is extolled by Captain Bonneville as the most enchanting he has seen in the far west; presenting the mingled grandeur and beauty of mountain and plain; of bright running stream and vast grassy meadow waving in the breeze."[16]

The first Fort Boise, built in 1813, was a Hudson Bay Company trading post. It was located near the present-day agriculture community of Parma, where the Boise River joins the Snake, north and west of present-day Boise. The Bannocks drove the trappers out the next year and again in 1819, but the British trading company returned in 1834. By 1836, the site was widely known as Fort Boise, and by 1843, it had become an important stop on the Oregon Trail. Indian resistance to the settlers continued, however, and in 1855, the post was abandoned. In 1862, the flood of the century washed the ruins away. The site is now owned by the Idaho Department of Fish and Game and protected as a waterfowl nesting area.[17]

Major Pinckney Lugenbeel founded modern Fort Boise on July 4, 1863, on what is now Fort Street in Boise's North End district. The location was at the crossroads of the Oregon Trail and the road between the mines in the Owyhee Mountains to the south and Boise Basin (Idaho City) to the northeast, where gold had been discovered the year before.[18] Miners took $250,000,000 in gold out of the Boise

---

14 Jim Witherell, *History Along the Greenbelt* (Boise, ID, privately published, 1990), p. 35.

15 Cort Conley, *Idaho for the Curious* (Cambridge, ID: Backeddy Press, 1982), p. 394.

16 Boise City Metro Plan, Adopted by the Boise City Council, October 1978.

17 Conley, *Idaho for the Curious*, p. 546-549.

18 Ibid, p. 394.

Basin in the 20 years that followed its discovery, more than the
California or Klondike gold rushes.[19]

No sooner had Lugenbeel picked his spot than Thomas Jefferson
Davis and seven others met at the Davis cabin on the Boise River and
diagrammed the townsite. That first version of Boise City consisted of
10 blocks that stretched from the Davis homesite to the new fort –
with five blocks on each side of the main street, which ran parallel to
the river. By the end of the 1860s, Boise had more than 400 buildings
and a population of about 1,000. Though originally a mining town, it
was agriculture that helped the city establish a more rooted economic
base. By the 1880s, more than 80,000 acres in the valley had been
turned for farming.[20] Davis would eventually own more than 1,000
acres, most of it along the river, including parts of what is now Boise
State University and Garden City.[21]

The river played a crucial role in this new economy. Tom Davis
was one of the first to divert Boise River water to irrigate the more
than 7,000 apple trees in his orchard,[22] part of which is now Julia
Davis Park. His success prompted others to follow suit.[23] In 1909, the
agricultural economy in the valley was stabilized when, after more
than 20 years of work, Diversion Dam and the 41-mile New York
Canal began to route large amounts of water from the river to irrigate
500,000 acres. A powerhouse was added below the dam in 1912, at
first to generate the power needed to build Arrowrock Dam upstream
and later for commercial and residential uses in the valley. The
engineer who surveyed Diversion Dam was Arthur DeWint Foote,
husband of author Mary Hallock Foote.[24] Her popular novel *The*

---

19 http://www.boisecounty.us/visit_boise_county.aspx

20 Conley, *Idaho for the Curious*, p. 167.

21 Witherell, *History Along the Greenbelt*, p. 82.

22 David Proctor, *The Idaho Statesman*, "Shared Legacy, July 23, 1989, p. 1D.

23 Andrew Putz, "Big Hearted River: The Life and Times of the Boise River," *Boise Weekly*, June 24-30, 1999, p.15.

24 Conley, *Idaho for the Curious*, p. 168-170.

Chosen Valley was a fictionalized account of the canal's construction.[25] In 1971, Wallace Stegner won the Pulitzer Prize for his novel *Angle of Repose*, which was loosely based on Mary Hallock Foote's life.[26]

In town, the Boise River witnessed a more urban type of development. On Warm Springs Avenue, investors built the Natatorium to take advantage of the natural hot springs in the area. The Nat was a glorious 150,000-square-foot, six-story entertainment complex that housed a swimming pool, a billiard room, café, roller rink, dance floor and formal dining room. When it was completed in 1892, it was the largest indoor natatorium in the country.[27] Though the building fell into neglect and was razed in 1934, a newer Natatorium swimming pool was later built nearby and named after its much more opulent predecessor.[28]

By and large, however, during the first decades of the 20th century, land near the pre-dam river was not seen as desirable property.

"When I came to Boise in 1929, the river was a lot of swampland," said Orland Mayer, an original Greenbelt Committee member. "There were no businesses there except for the (Chinese) gardens, and the land was constantly subject to floods. Of course, that was before Anderson Ranch Dam was put in, so the river itself was largely uncontrolled. There was an area there from Front Street over to the Union Pacific Depot (on both sides of the river) that was land that wasn't looked upon as good for business building; not like it is now."[29]

---

25 Witherell, *History Along the Greenbelt*, p. 7.
26 Boise Public Library brochure, printed 1999.
27 Witherell, *History Along the Greenbelt*, pp.52-60.
28 *The Idaho Statesman*, The Greenbelt: A Treasure Valley Labor of Love, p.2.
29 Orland Mayer interview with Troy Reeves, in Boise, ID; August 3, 1998.

The first parcel of developed land to become part of what would eventually be the Greenbelt was the Idaho Soldier's Home, now Veterans Memorial Park, located west of downtown on State Street at Veterans Memorial Parkway.

The home was the result of a national lobbying effort mounted by the Grand Army of the Republic, a fraternal group of Civil War veterans. The GAR's two major accomplishments were to secure a small pension for Civil War veterans and to invent the concept of soldiers' homes, a place to care for aged, poor or disabled veterans.[30]

Although Idaho was not yet a state then and had little role in the Civil War, the state had a strong GAR contingent thanks to the westward movement after the war. The GAR began to lobby for a soldier's home as Idaho approached statehood in 1890, and in 1893 the legislature approved $25,000. Walter Pierce, who wanted to sell residential land in the area, along with two other businessmen, donated 40 acres two miles west of Boise. The cornerstone was laid in May 1894, the building opened the first two floors in November that year and the official dedication came in June 1895.

The Soldier's Home survived 71 years, six wars and one major fire. At its peak in 1951, it held 132 veterans in a 130-bed facility. On November 11, 1966, the home closed its doors. The same day, the state opened the new Veterans Home on Veterans Administration Hospital grounds near the old Fort Boise.[31]

After some legal wrangling over the construction of the street that became Veterans Memorial Parkway, which was proposed to connect State Street and Chinden Boulevard, the Idaho Legislature in 1971declared the property to be a historic site and a state park. Veterans Memorial Park now comprises 200 acres, 76 of which have been improved. It is now a city park under a 25-year lease agreement with the state of Idaho.[32]

---

30 Witherell, *History Along the Greenbelt*, p.112.

31 Ibid, p. 119.

32 City of Boise website http://parks.cityofboise.org/parks-locations/parks/veterans-

In 1902, an era when most towns had their own amateur teams, the Instate League began to play organized baseball at the city's first private park. The triangular piece of land, located between Lee and River streets on the east side of 11th Street, was called Riverside Park. The ballpark held 1,000 fans, but on July 4, 1907, an estimated 5,000 people shoehorned themselves in to see Walter Johnson pitch for the Weiser nine.[33] Johnson's talent was already well known. Nicknamed Big Train, he went on to win an astounding 416 games in his Hall-of-Fame career for the Washington Senators, a team that finished under . 500 for more than half his 20 years there.[34] For a fee, park visitors could also enjoy an outdoor roller rink, a fountain, a gazebo and a dance pavilion. In 1906, the San Francisco Opera set up shop for three months after it lost its home to the-San Francisco earthquake.[35]

Cody Park, a new baseball field, was built in 1911 at Warm Springs and C Avenue, for Boise's Class C semi-professional team, the Boise Irrigators. Airway Park field was completed in 1939 in Municipal Park at Park Boulevard and Walnut Street for the Boise Pilots of the Pioneer League. The team later became the Boise Braves, and Airway Park became Braves Stadium. The stadium stayed in use until the Pioneer League folded in 1963. That property is now the site of the Idaho Department of Fish and Game offices.[36]

Julia Davis Park was the first public park on the future Greenbelt. Tom Davis donated 43 acres of his orchard on the north side of the river in his wife's name following her death in 1907, at age 60, from complications that followed a bout of typhoid she suffered a year earlier.[37] Though Davis required that "...the land would always and forever be used for public park purposes..."[38] the bequest was not an

memorial-park/.

33 *Boise Weekly*, Christian A. Winn, "Down by the River, Nov. 28, 2001, p. 10

34 Bill James, *The Bill James Historical Baseball Abstract*, (New York: Villard Books, 1986) p. 638.

35 Winn, "Down by the River," p. 10-11.

36 Witherell, *History Along the Greenbelt*, p.65-73.

37 Proctor, *The Idaho Statesman*, "Shared Legacy," July 23, 1989, p. 1D.

38 Boise Parks and Recreation web site, *Ribbon of Jewels*, http://parks.cityofboise.org/about-

immediate hit with the public, at least in a recreational sense. The land lay undeveloped and quickly became an illegal landfill. Judge Charles Winstead, chairman of the Boise Park Board, said in 1939: "The city accepted this ground in spite of protests and criticisms of our conservative citizens."[39] "Julia Davis was nothing but a city dump," recalled the late Bill Onweiler, one of the Greenbelt founders.[40]

So derelict and ignored was the property that it nearly reverted to the Davis Estate in the mid-1920s. Only a major civic improvement program, begun in 1926, saved the land for public use. The city later purchased additional acreage from the Davis family, and Morrison Knudsen Corporation donated riverside land it owned at the eastern end of the original Davis bequest. This allowed Julia Davis Park to expand to 89.4 acres from Capitol Boulevard, which was built in 1931, to Broadway Avenue. The Boise Zoo, now Zoo Boise, was established in 1920. The dumpsite was capped and the bandshell, now named after jazz pianist Gene Harris, was built over it in 1928. The Boise Art Gallery (now the Boise Art Museum) opened in 1938. Construction on the Idaho State Historical Museum began in 1940, stopped for World War II and was completed in 1950. More recently the park has become the home of the Discovery Center of Idaho and Idaho Black History Museum.[41]

What the Natatorium was to east Boise, Pierce Park, a private development six miles west of Boise's existing city limits, was to west Boise. At its peak in 1912, the attractions included a bandstand, refreshment stand, tennis courts, croquet plots, an artificial lake 250 feet wide and about three feet deep, and a dance pavilion.[42] Golfers at the Plantation Golf Course can now place side bets where Boiseans once gamboled.

us/ribbon-of-jewels/.

39 Proctor, *The Idaho Statesman*, "Shared Legacy," July 23, 1989, p. 1D.

40 Bill Onweiler interview with Troy Reeves, McCall, ID; June 19, 1998.

41 Witherell, *History Along the Greenbelt*, pp. 82-85.

42 Ibid, p. 130.

Pierce Park was part of a larger tract of land owned by the W.E. Pierce Co., which hoped the park would help the company sell homesites. The park succeeded, but the Boise Valley Traction Co. acquired the property for an interurban electric railroad that served much of the valley. Ownership passed to Idaho Power Co., then to the Plantation Company (which operated the dance pavilion). The park became Plantation Golf Course in 1932.

Ironically, Walter Pierce subsequently bought the Natatorium and the adjacent White City amusement park on the opposite side of town and competed against the park that carried his name.[43]

Municipal Park, the second major publicly owned park along the future Greenbelt, began life in east Boise as a vacant 23 acres off Walnut Street owned by the Boise School District. The district, which was then responsible for all public playgrounds, acquired the land in about 1910 to build a citywide intramural sport facility. That goal was never realized, and in 1918 the City Commercial Club leased the property and used it as a tourist campground and what amounted to a migrant labor camp.[44]

The need for such a facility was fueled by the recent increase in automobile ownership – and the resultant tourism it generated – as well as the rapid growth of the agriculture industry in southwest Idaho. Between 1912 and 1917, 12.7 percent of America's total farm growth occurred in Idaho.[45] The consequence was a large influx of motoring migrants looking for work and a new start. Without a controlled facility, the labor-seeking hopefuls were inclined to create tent camps in places they weren't always welcome. But at the Tourist Park they could use the communal kitchen with 14 hotplates, a laundry area with one washing machine, and a playground. A

43 Proctor, "A Shared Legacy," July 23, 1989, p. 1D.
44 Witherell, *History Along the Greenbelt*, p. 61.
45 Ibid.

bathhouse was added in 1919, which helped keep guests out of the river.[46]

To stay at the park itself cost nothing, but the Commercial Club charged visitors 25 cents per night for electricity. The first year, between June and October 1918, Boise Tourist Park served some 6,000 automobiles. The recession after World War I increased the migrant population and pushed usage up to 20,000 carloads; each car stayed an average of seven days. The traffic was too much for the Commercial Club to handle, and in 1927 Boise City bought the property from the school district and named it Boise Municipal Campground.[47]

Municipal Park, as it later became, served the traveling public – legally – until 1938. By this time there was an abundance of privately owned tourist parks that siphoned off the travelers who could afford to pay. This left Municipal and other similar public facilities for the hobos and "labor gypsies" whose numbers swelled during the Depression. In 1938, the city closed the park to camping and opened it to general use. A year later, Boise donated 11 of Municipal's acres to create the Airway Park baseball stadium.[48] Airway is gone now, but Municipal Park remained and became a crucial link in the Greenbelt. Immediately adjacent to the park, though technically not part of it, is the popular Morrison Knudsen Nature Center.

In 1926, Boise built its first airport on land that is now on the Greenbelt and owned by Boise State University. The year before, the federal government had created an airmail route that included Elko, Nevada; Pasco, Washington; and Boise. The Boise city council scrambled tof find land more suitable than the privately owned landing strips then in use. What the council settled on was a wedge of

---

46 Ibid.
47 Ibid, p. 63.
48 Ibid.

city-owned property near the river, west of Broadway Avenue, that was being used as a dump, plus 30 acres known as the Booth Tract. Booth Field was dedicated in January 1926. The runway was completed in March and mail service began in April. The hangars, finished in April, stood on what is now University Drive and Euclid Street. The brick and glass passenger terminal, perhaps the first terminal in the country of that construction, was finished in 1931. BSU's Bronco Stadium now occupies that property.

The biggest single event in Booth Field's short life came when Charles Lindbergh landed there on September 4, 1927, as part of his cross-country tour after his record-setting transatlantic flight earlier that year. Passenger service followed in 1931.

The city moved the airport to its present location, south of the city on Boise's second bench, in 1939, and sold Booth Field to Boise Junior College for $1.36. In more recent years disagreements over the Greenbelt easement through the Boise State campus sometimes strained the relationship between the college – now a university – and the city.[49]

Ann Morrison Memorial Park became the second major city park named after a woman. In 1958, Harry Morrison, co-founder of the famed Morrison Knudsen Corp., purchased 153 acres along the south bank of the river from the Boise School District and donated it to the city as a park. Morrison, whose company played major roles in the construction of Grand Coulee and Hoover dams, as well as in taming the Boise River, named the park in honor of his first wife, who had died the year before after a battle with leukemia. Though the property was valued at $1.25 million, it was not the user-friendly recreation spot it is today. The site was originally intended for a citywide high school, but the voters had turned thumbs down on two school district bond elections, and the property was subsequently neglected for years.

---

49 Ibid, p. 74-81.

In its original state, Ann Morrison Park was "overgrown with willows and cottonwoods, laced with sloughs and other soggy places."

Boise now had the land but no budget to turn it into a place anyone would want to visit. In response, hundreds of Boiseans contributed shrubs, trees, flagpoles and playground equipment, and the budget-conscious city parks department provided labor and extensive landscaping. When the city's rehabilitation costs exceeded the allotted $1 million, Morrison reached into his wallet and ordered crews to keep working. At his direction they added tennis courts, a clock tower, a playground and more landscaping. The parks department cleaned out most of the riverside vegetation, but retained about a hundred cottonwood trees and embarked on a tree-planting program. Today the park includes both shaded groves for picnics and shelter from the sun and wide-open spaces for soccer and softball fields, kite flying and Frisbee throwing. At the center of the park is a reflecting pool with water that cascades from an illuminated spray fountain.

The Harry W. Morrison Foundation deeded Ann Morrison Park to the city of Boise on June 7, 1959. The park, which stretches from Americana Boulevard almost to Capitol Boulevard, is popular year-round, but gets its heaviest use during the summer.[50]

West of Ann Morrison Park, across Americana Boulevard, is Kathryn Albertson Park. Its namesake, the wife of the late Joe Albertson, founder of the Albertsons grocery chain, lived in their home that overlooked the 41-acre park until her death in 2002.

---

50 Boise Parks and Recreation web site,
BOISEMagazineAnnMorrisonandKathrynAlbertson.pdf

The 1959 dedication of Ann Morrison Park. (Courtesy/Boise Parks &
Recreation Department)

Development of Ann Morrison Park in the 1950's. Note the increasing development in the sequential aerial photos. (Courtesy of Boise Parks & Recreation Department)

Originally, it was to be called just Albertson Park, but one night
Joe Albertson got a call at home from a woman who changed his
mind.

When Albertson told the story, repeating what the woman told him,
he hit his desk for emphasis: "'We've got (thump) Julia Davis Park!
We've got (thump) Ann Morrison Park! And that has to be Kathryn
Albertson (thump) Park!' I said, 'That's a hell of a good idea,' he
laughed. And that's how it came about."[51]

Similar in many respects to the land that became Ann Morrison
Park, the Kathryn Albertson Park property was an underused,
overgrown and often waterlogged horse pasture in 1979 when Joe
Albertson donated the land, valued at $3.6 million, to Boise City.
After they watched the land sit idle for nearly a decade, the Albertsons
– like Harry Morrison before them – chipped in another $1.5 million
for the landscaping, and Boise residents once again donated thousands
of trees and shrubs. As it happened, the park construction was
concurrent with the widening of the Curtis Road-to-Orchard Street
section of the Broadway-Chinden Connector – I-184 – that connects I-
84 to downtown Boise.

"Hundreds of large, spreading evergreens were spared from being
ripped out and (instead) were transplanted to the park," said former
Boise Parks Department director Jack Cooper.[52] The park today is a
home for resident and migratory wildlife, though it is located only a
few blocks from downtown Boise. Dedicated on October 17, 1989,
Kathryn Albertson Park features wide, paved footpaths winding
through the sanctuary, outdoor gazebos, a fountain, a cross-section of
the world's largest Ponderosa pine, glimpses of wildlife, including a
large population of nesting waterfowl, and access to the Greenbelt.

Subsequently, several Boise families continued the Davis,
Morrison and Albertson family tradition of donating parkland in honor

---

51   Proctor, "A Shared Legacy, July 23, 1989, p. 1D.
52   Cooper, written comments, April 9, 2001, p. 1.

of prominent women. Donated in 2003, Esther Simplot Park is 55 acres located between Main Street and Veterans Parkway on the north side of the Boise River near Whitewater Park Boulevard. It is set to open in spring 2016.

In 2005, Larry Williams donated 70 acres along the river, at the west end of Harris Ranch, for a park to be named after his wife, Marianne. The park contains two miles of Greenbelt pathway and a mile of river frontage.

Alta Harris Park, named for the wife of Dallas Harris who built the Harris Brothers Lumber Company and Harris Ranch, is 20 acres within what has become the Harris Ranch development. In 2015, the Thelma B. Lee Trust and the Harris Family Limited Partnership also donated three acres for a natural area near Warm Springs Boulevard and Parkcenter Bridge. The nature preserve is named for Golda Harris, wife of Ivan M. Harris.[53]

A 1.6-mile section of the Greenbelt's natural area is named for Bethine Church, an activist in her own right, daughter of Governor Chase Clark and wife of Frank Church who served four terms in the U.S. Senate. The 31.25-acre Bernardine Quinn Riverside Park is named for the wife of Maurice Harold Quinn, founder of the Quinn Robbins construction company and a lifelong Boise volunteer. The park is adjacent to the Greenbelt and Pleasanton Avenue, is dominated by the 22-acre Quinn's Pond. Amenities include fishing docks and open space.[54]

W hat makes these parks – and the Greenbelt – possible, at least in the way they are depended upon and used today, are the three dams built after Diversion was finished. The dams – Anderson Ranch, Arrowrock and Lucky Peak – regulate the

---

53 http://parks.cityofboise.org/news/2015/10/harris-family-donates-land-for-new-public-park-to-city-of-boise/

54 http://parks.cityofboise.org/about-us/ribbon-of-jewels/

flow of the Boise River and make it one of the "most nearly perfect flood-controlled rivers in the country," according to an Army Corps of Engineers official at the Lucky Peak dedication ceremonies in 1955.[55]

Boise, like most of southern Idaho and most of the West, has a desert environment. The arid southwest Idaho climate squeezes out only 11-12 inches of precipitation annually.[56] As a result, Boise's existence did and still does depend on captured water for irrigation and industry. Below ground it is held in the Western Snake River Plain Aquifer. Above ground the water is contained in a series of dam-created reservoirs fed by the Boise River, which is itself nourished by snowmelt from the surrounding mountains. And while the river did flood occasionally, it was the desire to hold onto this water and use it for irrigation that led to the first dams on the Boise, not flood control.

Boise experienced its first notable flood as a city 13 years after it was platted. Reports from the 1876 flood indicate it was not a particularly serious event. A few farmers were forced off their land and lost some topsoil and a few fences. The 9th Street Bridge washed out and cost $6,000 to repair, but no urban property damage was sustained. The Army Corps of Engineers estimated years later the peak discharge was 15,200 cubic feet per second, a fairly normal flood during the pre-dam era.[57] (A cubic foot per second equals 449 gallons per minute.[58]) Every 1,000 cfs pushed the river up its banks four to six inches.[59]

Two years later, a businessman named William Morris built the Ridenbaugh Canal, the first attempt to divert river water to the arid acres on the Bench, the land that rises on the south side of the valley – and the Boise River. The venture saw some success, but because it

---

55   Susan M. Stacy, *When the River Rises: Flood Control on the Boise River 1943-1985* (Boulder, Colo.: University of Colorado, Institute of Behavioral Sciences, 1993) p. xxi.

56   Ibid, p. xxii.

57   Charles Etlinger, *The Idaho Statesman*, "Boise River Speeds Up to Carry Water to Farmland," May 28, 2001, Local p.1.

58   U.S Geological Survey website http://md.water.usgs.gov/cfscalc/.

59   Stacy, *When the River Rises*, p. 108.

depended on natural flows, many of the farmers who used it suffered during low-water years.[60]

The river didn't rise again appreciably until 1896. In the meantime residential development had begun to pop up near its banks – what is now the Myrtle Street neighborhood. By this time, the city had bridges at 9th Street and at Broadway Avenue,[61] which allowed the construction of the first subdivision on the south side of the river.[62] By 1890, the valley population reached 10,000.[63]

The flood in May 1896 hit 35,500 cubic feet per second by actual measurement in the river.[64] High water washed out roads and threatened the old Broadway Avenue Bridge, but the flood plain at that time was mostly devoted to agriculture and the damage overall was minimal. The city had grown and learned how to cope with floods. Still, as historian Susan Stacy wrote, "One thing that hadn't changed was the deep regret with which farmers watched the floodwaters flow uselessly out of control to the ocean."[65]

The Carey Act of 1894, combined with the Newlands Reclamation Act of 1902, changed the West's economy irrevocably. The Carey Act allowed massive transfers of federal land to private farmers and offered economic incentives for eastern entrepreneurs to invest. The Reclamation Act provided the water to make those investments worth their while.[66] Land that had once been written off as hostile, useless desert became prime agricultural property. The Reclamation Act also gave irrigators throughout the West the tool they needed to be able to

---

60 Ibid, p. 6.

61 The replacement of the Broadway Bridge began in 2016. It necessitated rerouting of both auto Greenbelt traffic.

62 Ibid, p. 7.

63 Ibid, p. 10.

64 Ibid, p. 6.

65 Ibid, p. 8.

66 National Park Service website:
http://www.nps.gov/nr/travel/ReclamationDamsIrrigationProjectsAndPowerplants/Arrowrock_D am.html

capture some of that water – federal money. In 1909, the Reclamation
Service finished construction of Diversion Dam and the 41-mile New
York Canal. Known collectively as the Boise Project, the dam and
canal system diverted the Boise River from the dam, seven miles east
of the city. The water not used or lost in the journey filled the
177,000-acre-feet Deer Flat Reservoir, now Lake Lowell, where it
was used for storage and irrigation through the growing season.[67]

It took only 10 years for growth to overtax Deer Flat's capacity. In
1915, the Reclamation Service finished Arrowrock Dam 18 miles
above Diversion, just below the convergence of the Middle and South
forks of the Boise. At 350 feet, it was the tallest dam in the world.
More important, it stored 286,000 acre-feet of water.[68] Boise Valley
agriculture boomed. By 1920, the number of farms had grown from
1,600 to 4,800 comprising 374,218 acres.[69]

Like everywhere else in the nation, Boise's growth chart stalled in
1929 when Wall Street crashed and the Depression put a death grip on
America's economy. In the early 1930s, after years of drought and
overgrazed fields in the prairie states, farmers were hit by the Dust
Bowl. Even in Boise, with Deer Flat and Arrowrock reservoirs, "the
drought meant disaster for many," Stacy wrote.[70]

In 1937, the Bureau of Reclamation (formerly the Reclamation
Service) added five feet to the top of Arrowrock Dam and 30,000
acre-feet to its storage capacity. But farming by then had rebounded
from the drought years, and the additional storage was not enough to
support growing demand for water. In 1940, the Bureau of
Reclamation began construction on Anderson Ranch Dam, 42 miles
upstream of Arrowrock on the South Fork of the Boise. The Bureau
allocated 212,500 acre-feet of the dam's 500,000 acre-feet capacity to
hold floodwater, with the remainder dedicated to irrigation. World

---

67 Stacy, *When the River Rises*, p. 8.
68 Ibid.
69 Ibid., p.9.
70 Ibid., p. 10.

War II stopped construction – it was finished in 1950[71] – and the dam
had no role in the 1943 flood.[72]

That year, the combination of Arrowrock and Deer Flat proved
inadequate to handle the runoff from the above-average snowpack and
unusually high April temperatures. "At its peak, about 20,000 cfs
churned down the river," Stacy wrote. Downstream, farm families lost
crops and topsoil. Some 200 families, with livestock in tow,
abandoned their farms, and the Idaho Volunteer Reserves guarded
against looting. Authorities shut down all but three of the 14 Boise
River bridges for at least five days. Plantation Golf Course and other
land uses in the floodplain were inundated. The Corps of Engineers
estimated the damage at slightly less than $1 million.[73] Other
estimates were higher, but as Stacy wrote, "In summary, Boise Valley
managed the 1943 flood fight with no loss of life and little structural
damage in the city except for the bridges. The rural areas absorbed
most of the damage, with two-thirds of the $1 million in losses spread
across hundreds of flood-plain farms."[74]

After Boise dried out, flood-mitigation discussions included such
drastic remedies as widening, straightening, even re-forming the Boise
River so it had a broad, flat river bottom with high banks. Eventually,
however, even though Anderson Ranch Dam was not yet finished, the
Corps of Engineers and the Bureau of Reclamation decided that
Boise, then a city of 26,000, needed a third dam.[75]

The federal agencies got some help with their decision-making. In
1943, a group of heavy-hitting Boiseans created a new, private,
growth-oriented organization they named Southwest Idaho Water
Conservation Project, Inc., SIWCPI (or Sweepy-Weepy, as it was
popularly known). The president of SIWCPI was Harry W. Morrison,

71 http://www.usbr.gov/projects/Facility.jsp?
fac_Name=Anderson+Ranch+Dam&groupName=General

72 Ibid., p. 10.

73 Ibid, p. 10.

74 Ibid, p. 16.

75 Ibid, p. 29.

who in 1912 co-founded Morrison Knudsen Corporation with Morris
Knudsen. MK, as it is still remembered in Boise, later built enormous
reclamation projects throughout the world, including Hoover Dam.
Along with Morrison, board members included a bank president, a
county commissioner, a department store owner, a real estate
salesman, and agriculture magnate J.R. Simplot, founder of the J.R.
Simplot Company.

SIWCPI wanted to irrigate 200,000 acres in the Mountain Home
desert east of Boise. For that to happen, the government had to build
the Mountain Home Project, an elaborate dam and diversion system
that would have transferred water from the Payette River Basin to the
Boise River Basin. In the center of this plan was the proposed Lucky
Peak Dam and reservoir.

Clearly, the members of SIWCPI stood to gain enormously if the
Mountain Home Project were approved. The clout this group had was
equally undeniable. And it used it, together with the specter of the
1943 flood, to get the attention of Idaho's congressional delegation,
the Corps of Engineers and the Bureau of Reclamation. Harry
Morrison and Governor C.A. Bottolfsen sent telegrams to the Idaho
delegation and urged it to impress on the Corps how important it was
to take action to prevent a "disastrous flood next spring."[76]

The proposed earth-filled dam at Lucky Peak would hold 306,000
acre-feet of water and make 150,000 acre-feet available for irrigation.
It would also allow water from Anderson Ranch Reservoir to be sent
to the Mountain Home desert.[77]

SIWCPI did not get its entire Mountain Home Project, but it did
get Lucky Peak Dam. The principal reason SIWCPI failed was that
federal funding formulas required farmers who would benefit from the
Mountain Home water to reimburse the government for a portion of
the dam construction. By 1945, it became clear the farmers could not

---

76 Ibid, p. 24.
77 Ibid, p. 30.

afford the assessment. "It was $77 million too expensive," Stacy wrote.[78]

But when the Corps did the required cost-benefit analysis it showed the projected $11 million it would cost to build a dam at Lucky Peak would exceed the price tag of a flood by exactly $62,820.66. Something else had to be added to the equation. That something was the savings that would accrue to the still-unauthorized Mountain Home Project if Lucky Peak were built. In a convoluted bit of reasoning, the Bureau of Reclamation estimated Lucky Peak's water would be 85 feet above the level of the river, which was the level from which water would have to be pumped to supply the Mountain Home system if Lucky Peak weren't built. That reduction in the distance water would have to be pumped would save $85,400 in electricity. The Bureau also estimated if a power plant were built at Arrowrock Dam, the power sold would generate another $89,200. Add the recreation benefits and the $11 million Lucky Peak Dam made economic sense – at least on paper.

Later, when the Mountain Home Project was scotched and the Corps of Engineers eliminated the pumping-cost savings, Lucky Peak fell below the government's economic-benefit threshold by $1,290. In other words, the cost to build the dam would exceed its estimated benefits by slightly more than $1,000. Nevertheless, Col. S.E. Nortner, the Corps' acting division chief in San Francisco, determined the intangible benefits and the irrigation-related options for the future justified the project.[79] On July 24, 1946, with Arrowrock Dam still incomplete, President Harry Truman signed the $900 million Flood Control Act. One of its provisions authorized Lucky Peak.[80]

By 1949, before ground was even broken, Lucky Peak's cost had doubled to $22 million. In response, the Corps of Engineers campaigned for the dam by predicting better control of the river

---

78 Ibid, p. 32.
79 Ibid, p. 35.
80 Ibid, p. 36.

would allow more profitable use of floodplain land. When that wasn't enough, the Corps added in the value of recreation, supplemental irrigation and a reduction of downstream siltation.[81]

But for 25 years after Lucky Peak was built, the old, established riverside uses continued. Gravel was dug from the riverbank, cattle grazed on riverfront pastures, lumberyards and food processing plants contributed to the pollution. Eventually, of course, the floodplain did become popular and profitable, but probably not in the way the Corps officials foresaw.[82]

In 1949, the first Lucky Peak construction contracts were awarded and ground was broken. One of the large first-phase contracts went to Morrison Knudsen. Construction continued despite the Korean War, and George Roderick, President Eisenhower's undersecretary of the Army, dedicated Lucky Peak on June 23, 1955. Years later, Roderick's grandson and great-grandson, Ken Stolz Jr. and Robert Stolz, both served on the Greenbelt Committee.[83]

The only sour notes in this reclamation symphony were sounded by two Boise newspaper editors. In 1948, when the Corps of Engineers announced construction costs had doubled, the *Statewide*, a Boise weekly, posed the question: "Has there been, or will there ever be enough damage to Boise Valley farms to warrant the expenditure of $21.66 million? Wouldn't that much money buy nearly all the lowland farms, which might be flooded in the future? Would it stop a real rip-snorter anyway?"[84] In 1952, *Idaho Daily Statesman* editor James Brown described the Mores Creek Bridge as a "million dollar bridge to nowhere." He also accused the Corps of underestimating the cost of the dam only to "discover" later on that there would be a few additional costs. The next year he called Lucky Peak "a hoax."[85]

---

81 Ibid, p. 36-7.

82 Ibid, p. 67.

83 Ken Stolz Jr., interview with Troy Reeves, telephone interview from Missoula, Mont.; July 28, 1998.

84 Stacy, p. 41.

85 Ibid, p. 42.

What neither editor could have foreseen, of course, was the key role Lucky Peak Dam would play in the creation of the Greenbelt. The Corps of Engineers estimated in 1946 that, working alone, Anderson Ranch Dam would have controlled all but 21 of the floods that had occurred since 1865. With Lucky Peak in place, the dam system would have controlled all but two floods, "that is, held them to less than 10,000 cfs." The once wild Boise River was, if not broken, definitely harnessed.[86]

On one hand, the dams allowed residential and commercial construction along the river – which continues to this day – that would not have been feasible previously. On the other hand, the well-tempered river allowed the Greenbelt advocates to push the path through with only a little fear of flooding. "The fact that the dam is there is the only thing that makes (development to the banks) possible," said Alice Dieter, a member of the Park Board when the Greenbelt was created.[87]

The dams did not eliminate floods completely, of course. Portions of the Greenbelt still become unusable when the Boise gets its Irish up and flows at rates greater than 6,500 cfs. But the dams meant that while the Greenbelt pioneers had scores of other obstacles to overcome, at least serious flooding wasn't one of them.

---

86 Ibid, p. 35.
87 Alice Dieter interview.

2 People Just Didn't Care About the River

"It was just something you had to drive over."

– Jerry Tracy, park designer and project manager for Boise City Parks & Recreation

It was the Army Corps of Engineers, of all groups, that foresaw the changes Lucky Peak would engender on the Boise River. In 1949, when the first Lucky Peak construction contracts were let, the Corps predicted a completely harnessed river would permit a more "profitable use" than ever before of Boise's floodplain land.[88]

Of course, while the riverbanks have become some of the city's most valuable property, the sequence of events that created that increased value surely surprised Corps officials as much as it did everyone else.

It was recreation – the citizens' Greenbelt – that caused the dominoes to fall, not commercial real estate interests or government projects. It also took longer than the Corps probably thought – nearly 20 years – for those economic changes to take place.

The Boise River evolved rapidly throughout the twentieth century. Diversion Dam provided water for farms to the south and west of the

---

88   Stacy, *When the River Rises,* p.67.

city. Anderson Ranch, Arrowrock and Lucky Peak Dams harnessed the river almost completely.

The late Jim Kalbus, a Greenbelt Committee member, grew up in Eagle, downstream from Boise. For him, during the less industrialized years earlier in the century, the river was the place to be. "In Eagle, at that time, it was clear water and good," he said. "We used to catch bullfrogs, cut their legs off and Mother would fry them. Frog legs are very sweet, really good. But 40 years later that wouldn't have been possible because of the mess the river was in, even as far down as Eagle."[89]

That mess was created to a large degree by the law of unintended consequences. Through the 1896 flood, the 1920s drought and the Depression, agriculture continued to dominate the river bottom. During the 1930s, major floods on the Ohio River prompted Congress to make flood control a national issue. Part of that money spilled into the Idaho Legislature, which in 1936 allocated $10,000 for flood control work on the Boise River. The state highway department and the Works Progress Administration chipped in some more.[90]

The drive to control the floods led to construction near the river. The levees that flood-control money paid to repair made the river more predictable and safer to build near. As a result, land uses in the floodplain changed concurrently and became more permanent with each new flood-control project. The controlled river and the water from the dams made it easier to farm downstream. At that point, the dams combined with urban growth to absorb more farmland, while industrial uses moved into Boise and used the river as a sewer. The upshot was the second most polluted river in Idaho.[91]

---

89 Jim Kalbus, interview with Troy Reeves, Boise, Idaho; July 14, 1998.

90 Stacy, *When the River Rises*, p. 10.

91 Nate Johnson, *Boise Weekly*, "A River Runs Through It: The Paradox of the Boise River," July 30-August 5, 2003.

Pollution dumped into the Boise River, around 1966.(courtesy/Idaho Statesman)

"Eighth and Ninth streets filled up with warehouses and manufacturing establishments all the way to the bridge," wrote Stacy. "A number of gravel extraction operations mined the floodplain for its high-quality river rock."[92] What would become the Greenbelt was a strip of industries and amusements, railroads, gravel pits, packing plants, sawmilling, health spas and baseball.

In a 1994 article on the river's history, the *Wall Street Journal* reported: "By the early 20th century, the Boise River was a floating dump. On its banks stood sawmills and, later, slaughterhouses. A woman who grew up in turn-of-the century Boise once recalled the river smells of her childhood: dead fish, rotten bark and refuse."

"It really was the classic example of an urban river used primarily for waste removal," said Kevin Coyle, president of American Rivers, a national environmental group.

The state Health Department tested the water and concluded, "bacteria from raw sewage would present a definite health hazard to anyone who comes in contact with this water. Norway rats feeding on animal parts from the meatpacking plant were potential disease carriers."[93]

In June 1935, the city announced two new dumpsites – one at the south end of 14th Street and the other at the southeast corner of Municipal Park, both on the banks of the river.

Boise did attempt to pass bonds to fund a sewage treatment plant, but the bonds failed in 1938 and 1940. In 1947, a $1.55 million bond did pass, though it was more because people believed the pollution might cause polio than for other sanitary, aesthetic or recreational purposes.[94]

---

92 Ibid, p. 11.

93 Timothy Noah, *Wall Street Journal*, "The River That Runs Through Boise Runs Clear Once Again, April 22, 1994.

94 http://parks.cityofboise.org/media/947246/Urban-Research_May-2014_final.pdf

Ralph McAdams, who served on the Boise City Council from 1974 to 1986, described the river of his childhood as the receptacle for Garden City and south Boise sewage and the waste products of a slaughterhouse near what is now the Willow Lane Athletic Complex. When he wanted to wade in the river, he went in upstream from the zoo and the other dumpsites.[95]

Alice Dieter, an important early Greenbelt advocate and Park Board member, has similar memories. "The river was still pretty much a mess because we were hosing all the animal cages in the zoo into the lagoon, which is now the pond that people paddlewheel in, and that was flushed into the river," she said. "The storm drains in town were all dumping into the river. Then, in Garden City, you had packinghouses. It was pretty gross. People hadn't really thought of the river as an asset.

"My children used to ride their horses down to the river above Julia Davis Park, because it was clean there. And they used to play behind the Natatorium," said Dieter. "But by and large nobody paid much attention to it, except as a dividing line between north and south Boise. With only three bridges going across it, it really was a dividing line."[96]

As late as 1965, "you wouldn't think about swimming in it, tubing in it, fishing or anything," said John Heimer of Idaho Fish and Game.[97]

---

95 Ralph McAdams, interview with the author, Boise, Idaho, Dec. 1, 2000.

96 Dieter interview.

97 Nate Johnson, *Boise Weekly,* "A River Runs Through It: The Paradox of the Boise River," July 30-August 5, 2003.

Alice Dieter in 1981. She was named to the Park Board in 1964 and was a member when the Greenbelt was created. (Boise State University Special Collections)

That is not to say the river went without visitors or use.

Jerry Tracy, a park designer and project manager for Boise Parks & Recreation, remembered that in the 1940s and 1950s, adventurous kids fought their way through the briars and the brambles that bordered the river near Fairview Avenue, climbed the train trestle and jumped into the river. Some of the more daring "went all the way to the top and jumped over the power lines. The lines were closer to the bridge then," said Tracy, "but it must have been 50 feet to the water." The trestle, built in 1923, is now used for bicycle and pedestrian traffic.[98]

In 1959, the Jaycees sponsored the first "Keep Idaho Green" raft race and may have kicked off the popularity of tubing at least portions of the river. The *Statesman* described it as "the most disorderly race in the history of Boise."[99]

But most of the river was still unsuitable for play, and the riverbank was a home for hobos. Today, people still subsist along the river and under its bridges, though they are identified less romantically as homeless.[100]

"It's probably hard to visualize it this way now, but in the late 1960s and early 1970s, the river was pretty well trashed," said Elizabeth Van Zonneveld, the city's third Greenbelt coordinator, the staff person who worked with the Greenbelt Committee. "Every building near it used the riverbank as a waste ground. There were not many public access points to it; it was all private property.

"It was a concrete-dumping ground, piles and piles of old fences, refrigerators, trees and snags, trash, tires. It was the back door. Everything got shoved up against the riverbank and forgotten because it was not regarded as having any value. It was just a nuisance."[101]

"There were chunks of concrete, and there was a slaughterhouse," remembered Bert Cleaveland, who became a Greenbelt member in the mid-1990s. "You would go down the river and there would be chunks of lard or fat floating in the water."[102]

Ken Pursley, later a Greenbelt Committee chair, remembered seeing the river when he moved back to Idaho from Chicago in 1970.

---

98   Jerry Tracy, interview with author, Boise, Idaho, May 22, 2000.

99   Urban-Research_May-2014_final.pdf

100   David Collins, interview with Troy Reeves, Boise, Idaho; July 30, 1998.

101   Van Zonneveld interview.

102   Bert Cleveland, interview with Troy Reeves, Boise, Idaho; July 15, 1998.

As he drove across the Broadway Bridge, he said, "I was shocked to see a sign that said the water was not safe to swim in. It was because it was contaminated, not because it was fast flowing. I couldn't believe I'd come all the way back to Idaho to enjoy clear streams and an unpolluted environment, and the first thing I hit is a sign that says the water is too contaminated to safely swim in."[103]

Ken Pursley, in 1977. In 1975, as chair of the Greenbelt Committee, he helped dedicate Shoreline Park, the first official section of the Boise River Greenbelt. (courtesy/Idaho Statesman Archives, BSU Special Collections)

Jerry Tracy remembered what the Clements cement plant looked like for years before it became Shoreline Park in 1975. The old Wheels-R-Fun rental building, now owned by Boise Parks & Recreation, was the Clements company office. The tunnel behind the wooden building was built because there were so many spills from the batch plant it was easier to cover it over with dirt and grass and build a tunnel through it than blow up all the old cement. "Trucks would drive through and get batches of cement. A lot of it spilled," he said.

He also points to the gazebo that sits on the north riverbank, just south and west of the old cement plant office. It wasn't put there for aesthetic reasons. It was built to cover even more spilled cement. All one has to do is look over the edge to see a layer of cement that extends well into the river channel.

---

103 Kenneth Pursley, interview with Troy Reeves, Boise, Idaho; July 23, 1998.

"There was more concrete at the Boise Paving and Asphalt Company near where the Boise Fire Training Center is now," said Tracy. "Lots of spillage there, too."

By and large, the river "was just something you had to drive over," said Tracy.[104]

It didn't help that there wasn't much reason to cross the river in the first place. South Boise was not the place to be. "When I first came into the real estate business in 1951, nobody wanted to live in south Boise," said Keith Gilmore, a committee member from 1969 to 1971. "No one wanted to live by the river. That was for poor white trash. At that time, probably, the most expensive lots were if you had a view. Everyone wanted to get on top of a hill above the next person. The next trend was acreages. Everyone wanted an acreage. About the time the Greenbelt thing took hold, people started getting interested in living by water and along the river. All of a sudden the whole idea of south Boise turned around."[105]

Nevertheless, even into the 1970s, after the Greenbelt had begun to take shape and sewage treatment and some environmental controls were in place, there were places in the river people avoided. Historian Susan Stacy came to Boise as a junior planner for the Ada County Council of Governments in 1973. One of the first things she and a group of friends did was float the river in inner tubes. They had to portage around concrete and rebar. She also fished the Boise River and remembers a thick layer of slime near the Glenwood Bridge and downstream. "I didn't like to wade in those areas," she said.[106]

As far back as the 1950s, the city had made efforts to clean things up. Those attempts just didn't get very far. For years the river was the prize in a complex game of give and take,

---

104 Tracy interview.

105 Keith Gilmore interview, Troy Reeves, Boise, Idaho; July 15, 1998.

106 Susan Stacy interview with author, Boise, Idaho; Dec. 1, 2000.

clean up and dump into, during which the objective observer would have been hard pressed to know which side was winning.

Boise City stopped dumping raw sewage into the river in 1950, when the Lander Street Sewage Treatment Plant went on line. Five years later, Lucky Peak Dam made the river more aesthetically pleasing. It helped the looks but not the water quality.

Architect Charles Hummel grew up near the river in the 1930s and 1940s, and said that prior to Lucky Peak's construction the river was marred by its "gravelly scarred-out appearance." But once the flooding was under control, the forestry division of the Boise Parks & Recreation Department embarked on a campaign to line the river with cottonwoods. As a result, said Hummel, "The river has developed significantly heavily wooded sandbars and islands that didn't exist prior to Lucky Peak. And for that reason, in some ways the river has become more scenic. Prior to Lucky Peak there was no interest in floating or rafting the river because it was either too low to be interesting or too high and wild to be safe."[107]

Lucky Peak Dam turned the annual flood into a chapter in history. Seldom would 10,000 to 20,000 cubic feet of snowmelt per second rush out of the mountains to scrub out the river channel. Now, though the snowmelt could push the river to as much as 9,000 cfs, most years it was limited to about 6,500 cfs. Flows were steadier and more predictable. Vegetation was able to stick to the banks and shade trees could safely line the river corridor. Tubing the Boise River to Ann Morrison Park became a major summer recreation.[108]

To the west of Ann Morrison, it was a different story. That was where the price was paid for the aesthetics Lucky Peak had improved on the upper stretch of the Boise River. There, a new list of problems bubbled up. The Lander Street water treatment plant, on Boise's west side, treated its discharge with chlorine before piping it into the river.

---

107   Stacy, *When the River Rises*, p.68.
108   Ibid.

The dam-reduced water flows meant it was impossible to properly dilute the chlorine, especially since discharges were their highest during fall and early winter, when the river was at its lowest. Trout died. The low flows also encouraged the growth of the slime Stacy encountered when she went fishing. Though city funds built the Lander Street plant, there were no state laws at the time that defined water quality or that specified the amount of treatment waste must receive before it was discharged into rivers and streams.[109]

Former city council member and Greenbelt pioneer Bill Onweiler, who died in 2010, remembered Mr. Fletcher, the owner of the Fletcher Oil Company and a friend of Onweiler's father. The oil company was located at the end of Fletcher Street, which was right on the river. "All of the wire that had ever been accumulated, all the metal bands and junk and boxes, they would bring down Fletcher Street and put in his warehouse and then throw it out the back door."[110]

This was only the dawn of the ecology movement, what is now usually referred to as conservation efforts. The first Earth Day celebration was May 22, 1970, and environmental laws did not become part of the Idaho Legislature's agenda until after that. Without anyone at the Idaho Statehouse to tell them they had to, some food processing plants, dairies and other riverside industries were unwilling to invest in expensive settling ponds or treatment plants. Many still dumped their waste directly into the river, and detergents created mountains of floating foam.[111]

Biologist William Webb of Idaho Fish and Game found that the pre-Lucky Peak annual flood had acted as a spring-cleaning for the river, washing out the accumulated waste from the previous year. No flood, no cleansing. By 1959, Fish and Game reported the Boise was one of the two most polluted streams in the state. "In short," Stacy wrote, "Lucky Peak had created a river in which the banks became

---

109   Ibid, pp. 70-71.

110   Onweiler interview.

111   *The Idaho Statesman*, Greenbelt special section, p. 2.

more attractive, but the water flowing by them became much less so."[112]

On the plus side of the dam-and-water ledger, Boiseans thoroughly enjoyed the recreational activities Lucky Peak Reservoir provided. And in1959, when Harry Morrison donated Ann Morrison Park, it became an anchor for the Greenbelt concept and became the favorite take-out point for river floaters.

Amazingly, thanks to the city's continuing efforts, there are relatively few scars left behind to remind us of the real effort those visionaries put behind what has become a beloved amenity One exception is the cement visible at Shoreline Park, but even that is well disguised.

Things began to change in 1959.

---

112 Stacy, *When the River Rises*, pp. 69-71.

3 The Birth of the Greenbelt

"Things happen because people dream them."

– *Alice Dieter, Park Board member*[113]

Alice Dieter does not think there are any pat answers to the question of how the Greenbelt came to be. It was a complex process of individual decisions, of one person influencing another. And ultimately it happened, she said, because enough people wanted it.

"I believe things happen because people dream them," she said. "That may sound really weird, but if you don't have an expectation that something is possible, it clearly will not be, because you will not act to make it so. So I'm not being mystic when I say that. I've tried to sell a lot of different ideas in this town. I like causes, and I've been involved in a lot of things. This one you didn't really have to sell. There were people who didn't like the idea, and probably most of them went to their graves not liking it. But it was an idea that was easy for a lot of folks to share and to act in small ways and large ways

---

113 Dieter interview with Troy Reeves, in Boise, July 28, 1998

that made it happen. And to just keep at it, because it was the right thing to do. That's how it happened. There was no magic moment."[114]

Perhaps not. But there were certainly several key turning points: A close encounter with poison oak, an attempt to photograph the river, Boise's first comprehensive plan, a helicopter flight, a meeting with Senator Frank Church. And possibly most important, as Dieter points out, there was a series of individual decisions made by people in positions of influence who saw this Greenbelt idea was too good to ignore, and who were courageous enough to act on it.

One of the first of those was Boise printer Gordon Eichmann, who Greenbelt pioneer Stan Burns described as a "city wheel-horse,"[115] an old expression that described the horse closest to the front wheels of a vehicle – in other words, someone who got things done. Eichmann was president of the Capitol City Kiwanis club in 1959 and among the few in those days who dared to float the river in an inner tube. He knew the river's recreation potential. He also saw how difficult it was to reach the water through the jungle of growth that choked many stretches of the bank. Before the creation of Barber Park, he proposed the Kiwanis go up to Olson Manufacturing Co., a steel fabrication plant (later Gate City Steel) near the present site of Warm Springs Golf Club, to clear some of the poison oak so people could start their float there.

"Gordon Eichmann was the first to call my attention to it and say, 'Hey, let's look at the river as something other than just a nice view. People are using it,'" said the late Earl Reynolds, Jr., an engineer who was a Greenbelt Committee member intermittently from 1969 to when it disbanded in 1997 and then moved onto the Park Board.[116] Professionally, Reynolds served as chairman of the CH2M Hill engineering firm from 1980 to 1983. The company dedicated a bench

114 Ibid.

115 Stanley Burns interview with Troy Reeves, Boise, Idaho; July 7, 1998.

116 Earl Reynolds, Jr. interview with Troy Reeves, Boise, Idaho; June 18, 1998.

in his honor on the Greenbelt near ParkCenter Boulevard where he walked every day. Reynolds died in 2011.[117]

Architect Glen Cline, who designed the University Christian Church near Boise State, was another Boisean who early on saw what the river could offer. On a fall afternoon in 1960, Cline took a machete and hacked his way through the underbrush to the river to take photographs. What he saw through his lens that day was a river unfit for man or beast. Chemicals, concrete, grease, sugar beet pulp and animal blood were all part of the picture.

Glen Cline, an early Greenbelt proponent, in 1974. (Idaho Statesman Archives/BSU Special Collections)

But as it happened, Cline had recently read an article in an architecture magazine about a greenbelt, a strip of parks or undeveloped land, in New Jersey. In a flash, he made the connection between the greenbelt concept and the three parks that Boise already had along the river. He then made the leap to what could be. As luck would have it, Cline was then a member of the Boise Planning and Zoning Commission. For the next 18 months, Cline talked to friends and thought about the possibilities the river offered.[118]

---

117 Bill Roberts, "Former CH2M Hill chairman dies," *Idaho Statesman*, June 25, 2011.

118 Ellie Rodgers, *The Idaho Statesman*, "A Novel Idea Takes Root," Greenbelt special section, Sept. 28, 1999, p.3.

The early 1960s was the era in which the concept of land-use planning first began to seep into the consciousness of cities in the Mountain West. While Boise had long had zoning laws, there was no overriding document to guide the city as it grew. When Boise did begin its planning process, the first step was to create a comprehensive plan – a broad document that spelled out the goals that would guide the city's development for the next 20 years. The goals in the comprehensive plan would then become the foundation for the more specific planning and zoning ordinances. In May 1962, Mayor Eugene Shellworth and the Boise City Council hired Atkinson & Associates, a consulting firm from California, where land-use planning was not a foreign concept, to draw up Boise's first comprehensive plan.

Mayor Eugene Shellworth, 1961-65. (Boise City Department of Arts & History)

To familiarize himself with the city and determine what directions the plan should take, company principal Harold E. Atkinson undertook a series of meetings with the mayor and city council, city employees, and members of the planning and zoning board. One of those P&Z members was Earl Reynolds.

Atkinson saw potential in Boise that many of its residents had ignored or taken for granted. In December 1963, he handed his report to city officials. It urged them to do such things as enhance and protect the inherent dignity and beauty of Capitol Boulevard by retaining and beautifying publicly owned frontage; to retain the remaining park area around the State Capitol Building and consider developing an office building and mall complex north of the Capitol grounds; to maintain the Union Pacific Railroad Station as a community feature; and to identify and preserve public view sites along the highways both north and south of the city.

And Atkinson recommended the city acquire land along the Boise River to create a continuous "green belt of public lands" through the city.[119]

On April 26, 1964, the Boise City Council voted to adopt the Atkinson Plan as the city's comprehensive plan and with it the language that endorsed a "green belt." That endorsement, however, was not accompanied by any financial commitment. By state law, no Idaho city council can commit a subsequent council to future expenditures. It is a provision written to protect taxpayers, but it hampered Greenbelt development in the future.

"The Greenbelt was a great concept, still is a great concept," said Boise developer Peter O'Neill. "Except, administratively it was very difficult to do given the restrictions they had."[120]

Although others in Boise had talked about rehabilitating the river, it took an outsider to drive the point home. "It always helps when somebody comes in with a briefcase and says, 'You've got a jewel here that you better preserve.' Those words are more valuable sometimes than the local people's might be," said Earl Reynolds.[121]

The Greenbelt goal, just one item in Atkinson's long list of recommendations, caught a lot of eyes. Glen Cline, of course, noticed it. And by that time he had two avenues through which to pursue it. Not only was he on the Boise Planning and Zoning Commission, he was by then also president of the Capital City Kiwanis, an

---

119   Boise City Comprehensive Plan, p. 20.

120   Peter O'Neill interview with the author, Boise, Idaho, Jan. 19, 2001.

121   Reynolds Jr. interview.

organization that was always looking for community service projects.[122]

Reynolds saw the recommendation too. "It didn't take much convincing for me to see it was a great idea," he said. At the time, Reynolds was on the board of directors of the National Society of Professional Engineers. At a society meeting in San Antonio, he ~~had~~ had the opportunity to see the River Walk, a narrow two-and-a-half mile downtown park along the San Antonio River.

"At the time, the only greenbelt he could find was in San Antonio," said Bill Onweiler. "But it was so narrow the city workers couldn't get into it to pick up the trash. They had to float a barge down the river to pick up garbage."[123]

Boise, Reynolds realized, had the potential to do much better.

Gordon Bowen, director of the Boise Parks Department at the time, said his reaction to the idea was mixed. "I liked the idea, but I thought it was about 10 years too late to undertake such a project." He also knew that a greenbelt would cost money and feared it would take badly needed funds away from the new park acquisition program.[124]

Gordon Bowen in 1978. As director of the Boise Parks Department his support and organizational skills were crucial to the creation of the Greenbelt. (Idaho Statesman Archives, BSU Special Collections)

122   Ellie Rodgers, *The Idaho Statesman*, Sept. 28, 1999, p.3.
123   Onweiler interview.
124   Gordon Bowen interview with Troy Reeves, Boise, Idaho; August 5, 1998.

But Bowen decided to support the concept. Alice Dieter remembers that Bowen came to a parks board meeting with Greenbelt information already in hand. "(He) came to us and said he had already gone out and checked, and from what the city limits were at that time, one-third of it was already within public ownership or we could get a recreational easement from the (city franchised) water company," she said. "You had the (Boise) junior college campus, and you had the parks and this territory that was the state prison farm, which is now the (Warm Springs) golf course, and the water wells, and the railroad was still running back and forth where (some of) the path is now. So there were ways to get a recreational easement on about a third of the distance. He proposed that we set out to see if we could at least get a river setback ordinance."[125]

Dieter describes Bowen's approach as ponderously slow, but very caring and thorough. "He never got excited," she said. "He was always calm and steady, but he was relentless. He never gave up, and he never let a single detail fall by the wayside."[126]

His presentations may not have been stimulating, "but he was careful and methodical and thoughtful and a real gentle human being. He was just always there, doing his job."[127]

Nelson Miller, a Greenbelt Committee vice chair and a member from 1976 to 1982, said once Mayor Jay Amyx created the nine-member Greenbelt Committee in 1969, Bowen and the committee disagreed on only one basic design concept. Bowen wanted each tree to stand alone, while the committee liked more natural-looking clumps. Bowen liked grass and earth berms, the committee liked the natural look.[128]

---

125 Dieter interview.

126 Tim Woodward, *The Idaho Statesman*, "Walking the Greenbelt? Think of Gordon Bowen," Dec. 11, 1997, p. B1.

127 Dieter intervieew.

128 Nelson Miller interview with Troy Reeves, by telephone from, Seattle, Wash.; August, 17, 1998.

"There was the ongoing controversy between, should we dress it up and have mowed grass like Julia Davis and Ann Morrison parks or leave it natural?" said David Collins, a Greenbelt Committee member from 1973 to 1974.[129]

The Greenbelt Committee prevailed on most of those decisions. As part of the mayor's office, not the parks department, it had a little extra influence for its first 17 years. The Parks staff could speak at the meetings, but the committee didn't have to listen, said Nelson Miller. Under that arrangement, the committee could develop the Greenbelt sections the way it saw fit, then turn them over to Parks to maintain.[130] But Bowen eventually got his wish to pave the path.

Despite these differences, Bowen and the committee made remarkable strides together. Dieter calls him "the father of the Greenbelt. Without Gordon Bowen, we wouldn't have a Greenbelt."[131] Someday, she said, the city should erect Bowen's bust along this river.[132]

Bowen replied: "I don't consider myself the father of the Greenbelt. I consider (Harold) Atkinson in that role, with an assist from Arlo Nelson and Bill Onweiler. The role that I played consisted of mainly keeping the program moving. There were three Greenbelt coordinators in about three years. I provided the glue that kept the program from falling apart. That's what I consider my principal role."[133]

Stanley Burns was a Boise native who left Idaho for college and career but came back in 1953. He joined the Capital City Kiwanis and later became one of the original Greenbelt

---

129 Collins interview.
130 Miller interview.
131 Tim Woodward, ibid.
132 Dieter interview.
133 Bowen interview.

Committee members, but in the early 1950s one of his primary concerns was finding fishing buddies.

He joined the Ada County Fish and Game League and eventually became its president. Without realizing it, Burns had landed in the middle of a group with members such as Ted Trueblood, Ernie Day, Bruce Boller and Franklin Jones, outdoorsmen who became some of the most influential environmentalists in the West. In later years this group helped create such Idaho hallmarks as the Hells Canyon National Recreation Area and the Frank Church Wilderness. These men were concerned about what was happening to the natural world in Southern Idaho as far back as 1953-54. "Out of this organization came the desire to make the Boise River a place where kids could go and fish, which we used to be able to do," said Burns.[134]

Burns kept a letter dated May 28, 1964, written by the League to the City Council. It may have been the first public endorsement of the Greenbelt by an outside group.

The letter praised the council's vision and encouraged members to remember that the river is why settlers built Boise in the first place. "Is it not properly in the high interest of Boise's future that real regard be given to the priceless value and right use of our river?" the League wrote. "We feel the Council, in placing the banks of this stream for the entire length of the city under the protection of the designated Greenbelt, provides at once for the heritage of its citizens, not only a continuing resource of useful beauty but also a permanent tribute to the river for the city's real origin."

The League also asked that the Greenbelt be developed as a "full-length theme through the center of our community, showing to all that this is a capital city of unusual distinction."[135]

From there, the Greenbelt effort began to work like a multi-chambered heart – different components at work but with a common

---

134 Stanley Burns interview with Troy Reeves, Boise, Idaho, July 7; 1998.
135 Ibid.

goal. Civic clubs, equestrian groups, several branches of city government, private individuals, corporations and the federal government all became involved at different times and began to fit their individual pieces into the larger whole.

At about the time the Ada County Fish and Game League wrote its letter, Glen Cline and several other Kiwanis members had their organization moving in a similar direction but with even bigger ideas. Gordon Eichmann and other club officers realized Boise City did not have much money to spend on new parks. As Alice Dieter recalled, "The city had, at that time, never purchased a piece of park property. Everything they had had been donated."

In fact, Bill Onweiler contended the city allowed Morrison Knudsen Corp. to take over a large chunk of Municipal Park for a gravel pit "and never contested it."[136]

Dieter explained: "The city wasn't used to buying land for parks. And it didn't even make sense to a lot of people when you tried to talk about open space, because they were surrounded by open space. They didn't understand that they could become enclosed."[137]

Eichmann and other Kiwanis officials were aware of the city's mindset and financial situation. The Kiwanians thought, at least in a brief moment of innocence and idealism, that the club would be able to create the Greenbelt by itself.[138]

The club members already had one park construction success on their resume and were looking for more projects to undertake. "It's almost erased from history now, but as Lucky Peak Dam was completed and the reservoir was brought up to its present level, the club developed and built a little park up near Robie Creek," said Earl Reynolds, Jr. "At one time there was a bathhouse and an irrigation

---

136 Bill Onweiler, "Merry Christmas in 1987," unpublished, undated document, p. 4.
137 Dieter interview.
138 Burns interview.

system, some landscaping, to make it an attractive place for swimming."[139]

In July 1964, Burns received a letter from the Kiwanis Club saying he had been appointed to a special club committee. Also named to the committee were Glen Cline and Earl Reynolds Jr. It marked Reynolds' first official work on the Greenbelt, work that was to continue intermittently for 35 years. Dede Wilhelm, Jim Kalbus and John Chapman, all longtime Boise residents and later Greenbelt Committee members, are among those who point to Reynolds as one of the most valuable players on the Greenbelt team. "You couldn't find a greater asset than Earl Reynolds," said Wilhelm. "Earl, being an engineer, was so knowledgeable, but he was also so involved with people in the community," said Wilhelm. "He's a good pacifier of different sides, and he sees the picture beautifully."[140]

"Earl was a tremendous supporter of the Greenbelt concept, and I admire him today as well for his continuous working with the Greenbelt Committee and the concept of preserving the Boise River," said Chapman in 1998. "He's a tremendous man and certainly one of the fathers of the Greenbelt. I feel it a great honor to be among his friends."[141]

David Jones describes Reynolds simply as "Mr. Greenbelt."[142]

Not coincidentally, both Cline and Reynolds had earlier been appointed Planning and Zoning commissioners by Mayor Bob Day, a fellow Kiwanian. Those are two appointments of which Day was very proud.[143]

The new committee's objective, the Kiwanis letter said, was to "improve the conditions along the Boise River for the use and benefit

---

139 Reynolds interview.

140 Dede Wilhelm interview with Troy Reeves, Boise, Idaho; July 29, 1998.

141 John Chapman interview with Troy Reeves, Hailey, Idaho; June 15, 1998.

142 David Jones interview with Troy Reeves, Boise, Idaho; July 30, 1998.

143 Bob Day interview with Troy Reeves, Boise, Idaho; July 31, 1998

of all the people in our area." To that mandate, Earl Reynolds added
his own perspective. A former Oregon resident, he was familiar with
the way that state had preserved public access to its coastline. "That
was the main thing I was anxious to do; was to see that the public had
access to the river through the city," he said.[144]

The group met for the first time at noon on July 14, 1967, in the
old Hotel Boise. In a document titled "Kiwanis Club of Capital City;
Green Belt Committee; Proposed Outline of Committee Activity," the
group proposed to identify, as Bowen had, who owned the land along
the river and what it would cost to turn that land into a linear park.
The men who attended the meeting were identified only by last
names: Reynolds, McCarter, Eichmann, Cline, Burns, Frazier, Moon
and Belnap.[145]

Reynolds was heartened by the fact that the public already owned a
substantial amount of riverfront property.[146] But it didn't take much
investigation for the group to realize that while the goal was
worthwhile, the Kiwanis did not have the financial resources to make
it happen.[147]

Enter Bill Onweiler, Arlo Nelson and Sherm Perry.

The greenbelt concept had only recently been floated in 1963 when
Bill Onweiler made his first run for the Boise City Council. He lost
but came away from the campaign with a better understanding of what
Boise voters had on their minds. The two topics that had kept people
talking were urban renewal and parks. In 1965, Onweiler ran again.
This time, with his campaign managed by his wife, Corki, parks and
open space were the first two planks in his platform. Those issues, and
Corki's "genius for campaigning,"[148] helped him win that second race.

---

144 Reynolds interview.

145 Boise Parks & Recreation Department archives, Greenbelt time capsule, buried
September 30, 1999.

146 Reynolds interview.

147 Burns interview.

148 Onweiler document, p. 2.

In 1966, Onweiler became the council's liaison with the two departments that had been the cornerstones of his campaign – the Boise Parks Department and the city Planning Department. In that capacity he made the acquaintance of two city employees he described as "remarkable" – Parks Director Gordon Bowen and City Planning Director Arlo Nelson. Both men, Onweiler emphasized in 1998, played crucial roles in the early days of the Greenbelt.[149]

Nelson already had some Greenbelt experience under his belt by the time Onweiler arrived on the council. The planning director had drawn up a map that showed the river's path through Boise, Garden City and Ada County and had already held the first public hearing on the idea. To make sure people didn't miss his point, Nelson colored the riverbanks and existing parks a shade of red that could be seen from the back of the room.[150]

And it was a comment by Bowen, Onweiler says, that sparked his personal epiphany. "I was in a back room, talking about ways to prevent building in the floodplain. We were discussing it when Gordon came by and, with a twinkle in his eye, said, 'We could make it parks.' The Greenbelt was born in that moment."[151]

Onweiler then looked at the practical aspects of the situation and saw a political solution to the question of how to make the Greenbelt idea work. He knew the Army Corps of Engineers had just completed a new study that mapped the Boise River's 100-year floodplain. He was also aware Arlo Nelson wanted to keep people from developing in the floodplain. And he knew Bowen was looking for land the city could set aside for parks.

"Well, what better way to use (the floodplain) than parkland?" asked Onweiler. "If you flood it, the grass isn't going to die. (The Greenbelt) was a good alternative to permanent development. And it

---

149 Ellie Rodgers, *The Idaho Statesman*, "The Community Pitches In," Greenbelt special section, September 28, 1999.

150 Ibid.

151 Tim Woodward, *The Idaho Statesman*, Thursday, Dec. 11, 1997.

happened to tie all of the parks together. It was a perfect fit for all three guys."[152]

In a second brainstorm, Onweiler decided to sell the Greenbelt idea to citizens, not other politicians. He calculated that if the people wanted it, they would figure out a way to do it.[153] His job, as he saw it, was to make them want it.

To do that, he began to work with the late Sherman Perry, a fellow council member and Greenbelt advocate who would later become council president. Perry, Onweiler said, was "the only city councilman that understood what I was trying to do."[154] He and Perry decided they would go where the people were. They started with Boise's abundant civic clubs to see if they could be convinced to support the Greenbelt. The first presentation was at the Lions Club where Onweiler was a member and former program chair.

Most service clubs liked a 20-minute presentation – 10 or 12 minutes of talking with a question-and-answer period. At the Lions Club, the interest was so intense Onweiler had to shut off the questions after 20 minutes. "...I knew I'd struck a civic nerve," he said.[155]

---

152 Onweiler interview.
153 Ibid.
154 Ibid.
155 Onweiler document, p. 5.

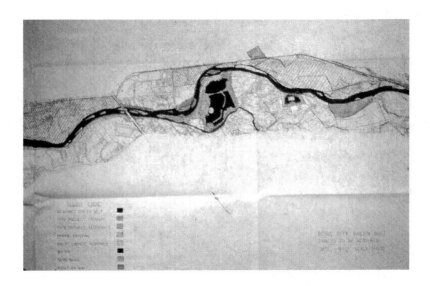

Gordon Bowen's 1971 map. Tracts acquired or desired are in gray.
(image/Boise Department of Parks & Recreation)

He and Perry had Nelson's map, but Onweiler wanted something
even more dynamic to show the clubs. From KBOI-TV owner Wes
Whillock, he borrowed City Hall reporter and photographer Garth
Andrews. At the Boise Airport, he enlisted the help of airport manager
Don Duvall,[156] who also happened to be a member of the Idaho Air
National Guard and needed flight time to keep his rating as a
helicopter pilot. It was only a two-man chopper, so Onweiler had to
stay behind. At five o'clock one morning in 1970, Duvall and
Onweiler strapped Andrews up "and hung him out the side of the
thing," said Onweiler. The photographer and the pilot flew the length
of the proposed Greenbelt and back in less than an hour.[157] Onweiler
and Andrews took the raw film and used the TV station's cutting room
to edit it down to just less than nine minutes and create a coherent

---

156 Ellie Rodgers, *The Idaho Statesman*, Sept. 28, 1999, p.4
157 Onweiler document, p. 6.

story. Onweiler wrote a script, and Andrews found some music to put behind it.

"It was the most amateur work you probably ever saw. And as it turned out, it was the most influential thing that, I think, was ever shown in Boise," Onweiler said. "Maybe because it was so damn hokey." He added, "The people in Boise had never viewed their river from this angle. In fact, most never saw where the river flowed within the city."

Onweiler's self-criticism is a little harsh. Given what he had to work with, the result was a tight, effective propaganda film. He started his narration by pointing out it was the river that created Boise in the first place by attracting the pioneers to the valley nearly 200 years before. Today, he continued, the river bisected a city of 75,000 people, flowing from the Barber Valley on the east, past Municipal Park, Julia Davis Park, Boise State College and Ann Morrison Park, then left Boise between the Plantation Golf Course and the Western Idaho Fairgrounds.

With canned, pseudo-bossa nova music in the background and a slow-motion aerial view of the river rolling by on the screen, Onweiler briefly recounted the recommendation of the Atkinson Report and the city's recent riverside property acquisitions. "Boise is well on the way to acquiring a continuous public strip through the city," he said.

Onweiler argued in his narration that the Greenbelt would be, what is called today, a win-win. If the riverside land were preserved for public use "forever" and the adjacent land available for private development, the resulting linear park would feed the desire for local recreation near water and encourage needed tourism and commercial construction, he said.[158]

---

158 Bill Onweiler, Boise Greenbelt promotional film, 1970, Boise, Idaho. https://www.youtube.com/watch?v=dskPRdi2k9I&feature=player_embedded

What he didn't describe, what he let the pictures show, were the harsh industrial uses the often denuded banks of the river were then being put to. In the fall of 1970, Onweiler and Perry took the film and hit the civic club circuit, "Together, we made a hundred of them," Onweiler estimated. "God, we used to do two or three a week."[159]

At each meeting, Perry would talk for seven or eight minutes about the Boise of his childhood, how he used to deliver newspapers for spending money, how for fun he used to grease the trolley tracks going up Americana Boulevard, and how he came to know "every nook and cranny of this town," Onweiler said. Perry could get quite emotional about it. "You could almost see the tear in his eye," Onweiler said. Then Onweiler would show the film of the Duvall-Andews flight. The response was overwhelming. "An hour later we would still be answering questions," he said.[160]

"I had people who actually had lived in Boise two or three years who were unaware that there was much of a river that ran through town. They just drove across the bridges. They didn't look in."

While Onweiler's one-note outspoken advocacy and political relentlessness would come back to bite him, it paid off early on. The Onweiler-Perry speaking-and-film campaign worked. "I was surprised to find that the concept proved very popular with Boise citizens, and there was soon talk about how to implement it," said Gordon Bowen. There was opposition from the riparian property owners, some of whom feared the Greenbelt "would provide a hangout for hippies, mooners and ne'er-do-wells," wrote Bowen. Others had plans of their own for development or use of the riverbanks. But some property owners who were strong supporters even donated Greenbelt property to the city.[161]

---

159 Oneweiler document,
160 Ibid.
161 Gordon Bowen, *Boise Parks: A Cause and Trust*, 2002, p. 143.

While Perry and Onweiler sold the idea to the public, Bowen championed the idea within the city government. The city Planning and Zoning Commission, park board and parks department embarked on their own study to define the Greenbelt, examine land ownership and determine the project's feasibility. The Planning and Zoning Commission held the first public meeting on the Greenbelt idea on December 28, 1965. Park board members were invited.

4 From Vision to Reality

The Greenbelt setback "was one of the biggest political battles we fought."

– John Chapman, former Greenbelt Committee chair

In 1966, the Greenbelt became more than just a closely held idea. A citywide discussion was underway, and city officials began to take tangible political action.

The approval process for the Greenbelt and the accompanying property setback began on January 20, 1966, when City Planner Arlo Nelson made a presentation to the park board. Using his aerial map of the river and adjacent lands within the city, he pointed out which properties were city-owned, and what might be acquired by Boise, Garden City and Ada County.[162] The staffs of the three governments estimated it would cost $945,000 to acquire up to 42 needed pieces of property.[163]

Later that month, the city council strengthened the pro-Greenbelt comprehensive plan statement when it passed a resolution to make the Greenbelt an official city goal.[164]

---

162 Stacy, *When the River Rises*, p. 74.

163 Gordon Bowen, *Boise Parks: A Cause and Trust*, 2002, p. 143.

164 Ibid.

In September, the council, at Bill Onweiler's urging, made one of the most important decisions in the history of the Greenbelt when it passed Ordinance 3240. It was the Greenbelt's Declaration of Independence. The ordinance not only officially defined the Greenbelt, it established a setback. No building would be permitted within 50 feet of the 6,500 cubic-foot per second line, or 20 feet from an existing Greenbelt boundary.[165] The city used the 6,500-cfs line as drawn by the Army Corps of Engineers, said historian Susan Stacy, Boise's former planning director, because that was an average high-water mark.[166]

"In order to keep people from building down to the water's edge, and over the water, we felt there should be a setback to preserve the Greenbelt space and allow enough of a Greenbelt area to provide access for pedestrians and people to walk along the river," said John Chapman, who chaired the Planning and Zoning Commission at the time and later became chair and member of the Greenbelt Committee.[167]

The setback became part of the first Greenbelt ordinance in 1971. In 1978, the ordinance was amended to increase the setback to 70 feet from the 6,500-cfs mark or five feet from the boundary of all dedications or easements granted to Boise City for Greenbelt purposes in excess of 65 feet.

On Oct. 31, 1966, a month after the council passed Ordinance 3240, the Idaho Department of Parks and the city of Boise agreed to create a greenbelt from the middle of Julia Davis Park to Capitol Boulevard. It was sometimes referred to as "The Little Greenbelt," and work was completed in 1967.[168]

---

165 Wayne Gibbs email to author, December 26, 2000.
166 Stacy interview.
167 Chapman interview.
168 *Greenbelt Resource Book.*

The city acquired its first land specifically for the Greenbelt on Dec. 12, 1966, when the council voted to vacate 0.43 acres of Owen's Lane, north of the Main Street Bridge.[169]

As the city grew, so did the Boise Metro Plan. In 1985, the plan was amended again to include the newly written Boise River Plan. To provide a corridor for wintering bald eagles, the river plan mandated a 200-foot setback from the 6,500 cubic-feet-per-second flow line on the east side of Boise, upstream from Walnut Street on the north side and upstream from the fourth phase of the River Run subdivision on the south side. Though this planning goal was applied to later developments such as Spring Meadow, it was not set forth in an ordinance until the adoption of the Boise River System Ordinance in 1993.

But it was that first setback ordinance that became the cornerstone of everything that came after and gave the Greenbelt an important anchor point on which to build. By 1983, the Greenbelt comprised about 75 acres and eight miles of paved path. It linked six parks and the Warm Springs Golf Club, though the paved path to the golf course was not finished until 1990.[170]

"That setback really saved the whole concept of the Greenbelt," Chapman said. "We never could have afforded to buy that access if it had been covered by multi-million dollar apartment buildings or restaurants. As it was, we were able to halt the development in the Greenbelt strip and the access areas, which allowed us ultimately to acquire and approve the Greenbelt for the public's use. It was the high point of my involvement."[171]

As word of the city's plan spread, many property owners along the river screeched like scalded cats.

---

169 Chapman interview.
170 Gordon Bowen, written comments, p.1, August, 23, 2001.
171 Chapman interview.

"Initially, there was a hue and cry because the concern was that the bureaucrats and the government were going to take over private land along the Boise River," said Stan Burns, somewhat facetiously. "Naturally, we wouldn't want any bureaucrats telling us what to do with our land. Prior to that it had been wild country. If you had a load of trash, you would take it down to the river and dump it. If you had a cement truck that had half a load of cement in it, you'd take it down and dump it in the river."[172]

But if the riverside property owners had looked at their own history, they could have predicted that development, and increased land values, would follow the Greenbelt. Just as the geothermal development and the Natatorium in the 1890s spurred the growth of Warm Springs Avenue, and the Hillcrest areas on the Bench and Pierce Park grew when trolley lines were built about 1905, public access means demand increases and prices follow.

But not everyone is a student of history. "I remember distinctly walking up a path to a guy's house to talk to him about his land and the possibility of public access," said Elizabeth Van Zonneveld. "He met me at the gate, not at the door, with a shotgun. He pointed it at me and said. 'This here is my land, and I'm keeping it.

"That was a really good example of how people felt about their land ownership. But we persevered. We talked to one owner after another and explained how the public development of river access would be beneficial to the property owners in the commercial part of the city. We picked up the easy ones when we could and kept knocking on the doors of people and businesses who weren't cooperative."[173]

"I remember some people being very concerned when they first heard of the (setback) ordinance, that it was going to lower the value of their land and they wouldn't be able to sell it or do anything with

---

172 Burns interview.

173 Van Zonneveld interview.

it," said Ken Stolz Jr., a committee member in 1976. "I found it ironic that shortly after it passed, the value of all the riverfront properties quadrupled overnight."[174]

"It was one of the biggest political battles we fought, and we did a lot of work to get people's support," said John Chapman. "It was not easy to convince people in those days that passing the Greenbelt ordinance would improve Boise. We took various members of the council to lunch and talked to people and put on programs at civic clubs. It was an uphill battle in those early years, but now it's one of the most valuable projects the city has ever entered into."[175]

On January 26, 1966, the lobbying paid off. The Boise City Council adopted the Boise River Greenbelt Plan in its entirety as a joint resolution from the Planning and Zoning Commission and the Board of Park Commissioners. It was only a "statement of policy, of future intent with regard to the Greenbelt," said Gordon Bowen, but it put on the record the city's intent with regard to the Greenbelt and gave Boise the leeway to acquire property as it became available.[176] Humble as it may have been, the action put the setback on the books and the Boise River Greenbelt became an official city goal.[177]

Over the next decade the city developed a set of guidelines for the Greenbelt's expansion.[178] Included in those guiding principles were instructions that the city preserve for the public unrestricted access to the river and the recreation it provides; preserve the river's aesthetic, wildlife and educational values; minimize water pollution; use the river as a buffer zone between business and industrial uses and government, education and residential uses; provide continuity for such recreational uses as hiking and riding trails; define and delineate

---

174 Ken Stolz Jr. interview.
175 Chapman interview.
176 Bowen, written comments, p.1.
177 Stacy, *When the River Rises,* p.74.
178 Cooper, written comments, p.2.

floodplains and restrict permanent construction there; and provide a framework and environment for outdoor recreation.

But January 1966 was the middle of the budget year, and no funds were allocated to the project.[179] That pattern – lip service and some important votes for the Greenbelt but a reluctance to fund it with city money – was one Boise City government repeated for the next 30 years.

This still is not an unusual way for Boise to operate. Because this relatively small city is and has been the home of the J.R. Simplot Co., Albertsons Inc., Morrison Knudsen Corp., Micron Technology and a large Hewlett-Packard presence; because the residents are often reluctant to tax themselves with bond issues; and at times because of revenue restrictions imposed by the Idaho Legislature, the city often has ignored a need until a white knight stepped up to pay for it.

Boise held the title to the property that became Kathryn Albertson Park for nearly a decade. Only when its donor, Joe Albertson, put up $1.5 million, did the city create a park out of the neglected horse pasture. Ann Morrison Park, the Morrison Center for the Performing Arts (both received major funding from the Harry Morrison Family Foundation), and the Esther Simplot Performing Arts Academy and the Esther Simplot Park (funded by the family of agriculture and computer chip magnate J.R. Simplot) are three more examples of needs that were met by patrons, not by the city or bond issues.

The Greenbelt had no such patron. It was created in the imagination of volunteers and pieced together in halting, painstaking fashion with easements, vacated right of ways, conditional uses that were traded for donations or easements, land swaps, condemnations, donations from individual property owners, federal conservation and recreation funds (including money from the Intermodal Surface Transportation Efficiency Act), government grants and matching funds from city and state.

---

179 Stacy, *When the River Rises*, p. 158.

The city's miserly fiscal policy did not escape the attention of Greenbelt Committee members. As Joe LaMarche (Greenbelt Committee 1983-87) pointed out in 1998: "I'm always amazed by the fact that the politicians in town loved to claim ownership of the Greenbelt but still are terribly reluctant to really fund it sufficiently to assure that there is money for maintenance and so forth to sustain it. That bothers me."[180]

Alice Dieter noted that at the time she was appointed to the park board (by Mayor Eugene Shellworth in 1964), the city had yet to purchase its first square inch of park property. In fact, the park board was giving away land, Dieter said. The Naval Reserve offices in Julia Davis Park were leased at a very modest rate to the Discovery Center of Idaho. Elks Rehabilitation Hospital was given park property from the Fort Boise Reserve. Boise Little Theater, the Boy Scouts and the Girl Scouts were likewise all given parkland.

"I used to say, 'I'm a peasant,'" Dieter said. "I don't believe in giving away land."[181]

On February 7, 1966, *Idaho Statesman* reporter Bob Lorimer offered this description of the proposed Greenbelt and the setback: "It would provide an eventual, uninterrupted strip of land alongside the Boise River that could be used in the interest of health, welfare, and recreation. The belt will be particularly beneficial in providing hiking, picnicking, camping, nature study, bicycle and horseback riding, fishing and water sports, to a wide range of users and will contribute priceless aesthetic values to the community.

"It is expected that the belt will eventually be able to extend to Barber Bridge, east of Boise, to the area of the Old Soldier's Home on the western outskirts of the city (Veterans Park). It is hoped that the belt will be able to maintain a minimum of one hundred feet in width

---

180   Joe LaMarche interview with Troy Reeves, Boise, Idaho; July 22, 1998.
181   Dieter interview.

along the river, with some spots offering side stops several acres in size. However, at some critical points in the increasingly valuable industrial and business areas, this may be decreased to as little as thirty feet, or even narrower."[182]

Lorimer's qualifying language – "It is expected." "It is hoped" – marked a recognition of reality. Several giant steps had to be taken before the Greenbelt could become more than merely a paper goal. Opposition from some landowners and politicians had to be overcome. Money for acquisition and maintenance had to be found. And questions of exactly what the Greenbelt would be – park or path, and if horses and bikes would fit in the mix – had to be resolved.

As so often happens, it was the vision of money that converted the doubting politicians who initially opposed, or were at least cool to, the Greenbelt idea. "What finally won the day was the concept of how valuable this Greenbelt would make the adjacent lands," said Stanley Burns. "Once the city council got the message that these would be taxable properties of considerable value, whereas at the present time the land was worth virtually nothing on the tax rolls, and when developers could see the opportunities of having condos, apartments and various things along the Boise River, then it started catching hold."[183]

The debate was still years from over. Developers and other landowners would have a lot to say about the path as it began to stretch through the city and into Ada County. But the Greenbelt was at least given a chance to take its first halting steps toward proving itself.

Burns also offered another of his many helping hands by finding a funding source. A friend of his, Maury Lundy, was a Seattle-based biologist and wildlife specialist in charge of the U.S. Bureau of Outdoor Recreation. Burns wrote to him about the Greenbelt, and Lundy loved the idea. In July 1970, the city purchased three parcels

---

182 Bob Lorimer, *Idaho Statesman*, February 7, 1966.
183 Burns interview.

between Americana and Capitol boulevards with Bureau of Outdoor Recreation matching funds.[184] Over the years, Lundy and the Bureau of Outdoor Recreation managed to funnel a lot of money into the Greenbelt.[185]

"Basically, most of the action in those days was between Capitol Boulevard and Americana (Boulevard)," said Morgan Masner. "We thought that if we could ever get a greenbelt between Capitol Boulevard and Americana, we would have really accomplished a lot. And we pretty much did on one side, on the south side. Fortunately, Ann Morrison Park was there. There was a lot of cleanup needed over there. But once we got that done, and once people used it and saw what it was and walked on it and understood what was going on, it got easier and easier and easier and easier, to the point where there were attempts to give the city more (land) than really the city could take on.[186]

"As we got rolling, the only political problem was if you didn't support it," said Earl Reynolds, Jr.[187]

The Greenbelt appeared to be a winning proposition for everyone – except the equestrians.

The early support of horse owners, many of whom had ridden for years along the river where they could find access, was among the first spurs to Greenbelt development. While some Greenbelt pioneers in retrospect question Mayor Jay Amyx's commitment to the Greenbelt, where his daughter rode, Keith Gilmore, an original Greenbelt Committee member, thinks the idea of a bridle path was crucial in swaying the mayor into the "Yes" column.[188]

---

184   Greenbelt Committee minutes, July 6, 1970.

185   Burns interview.

186   Morgan Masner interview with Troy Reeves, Eagle, Idaho; June 10, 1998.

187   Reynolds Jr. interview.

188   Keith Gilmore interview with Troy Reeves, Boise, Idaho; July 15, 1998.

Orland Mayer, another original committee member, said, "In those days there was a group of people in Boise who enjoyed morning rides with horses, and one of the things they said was, 'Well, this will be fine, a path where we can take our horses in the morning.' This started up quite a little opposition from other people because of the problem of horses going on it, both because of the hazard and because of the manure problems involved. You will notice in the (original) plan they did provide an area for horses, but it never was developed at all."[189]

Ken Pursley, an early chair of the Greenbelt Committee, lists the lack of an equestrian right-of-way as one of his few regrets about the Greenbelt. "I like horses, I like to ride horses," he said, "and I was sad that we were never able to build a horseback trail into any section of it, because that was one of the original uses in the original plan. But you have to have a lot more width to do that."[190]

The conflicts between the different types of users – horses, pedestrians, roller blades and bicycles – have been part of the Greenbelt since its conceptual stages and only grew once the path began to be used. But more basic even than the horse debates was whether the pathway would be paved. "We didn't want a hard surface initially," said Stanley Burns. "Many of us, particularly Art Troutner, who was the prime mover in Trus Joist, were adamant that it shouldn't be a hard surface, that it should be soft material."[191]

Burns wanted a soft surface of wood chips on dirt similar to what Eugene, Oregon, would later build and name Pre's Trail, after the late Olympic runner Steve Prefontaine.

Burns feared the Greenbelt would become "a bicycle thoroughfare up and down the river." His vision was of "a natural, quiet trail that would be good for families and walking and hiking and running enthusiasts on the river. It was a great sadness to find our fears

---

189   Orland Mayer interview with Troy Reeves, Boise, Idaho; August 3, 1998.
190   Pursley interview.
191   Burns interview.

became true, and now the Greenbelt is one of the popular
thoroughfares for people on bicycles to get to the city. I think that is a
problem that sooner or later will be addressed by a substantial lawsuit
brought against the city for their lack of supervision of that activity,
because pedestrians and bicycles going 20 or 30 miles per hour are not
congenial. We tried to forego that, but because of politics and
weakness of some of our elected officials we lost out to the
bicyclists."[192]

Elizabeth Van Zonneveld succeeded Bill Onweiler and Gay Davis
as Greenbelt coordinator and was the first to be paid. She recalled that
a bike path was not a major part of the original conception. "Since that
time in its development, bike paths and walking paths have become
very important features of it. But originally, I think, most of the
people who were interested in it, and were trying to support it, were
really thinking of it in terms of open space, the preservation and the
quality of the river and making it accessible to the public."[193]

But there were two strong forces at work to get the path paved.
One was bicyclists. The other was Gordon Bowen, director of the
Boise Parks Department. Burns described Bowen as "a very good
man," but one whose concern about how his department would
maintain the Greenbelt motivated his decision to support the paved
path. "He foresaw that unless there was a hard surface they couldn't
run those trucks and maintenance vehicles up and down the Greenbelt
very well, so he went for asphalt," said Burns. "Asphalt, of course, is
directly in opposition to what we know to be good for fresh water. The
runoff over asphalt carries a great number of contaminants and in the
case of the Greenbelt goes right into the river, which is dead
wrong."[194]

---

192 Ibid.
193 Van Zonneveld interview.
194 Burns interview.

The actual paving didn't start until about 1974, when the city tackled the stretch from Capitol Boulevard to Americana Boulevard.[195] Knowing the problems associated with asphalt, the first paving material was a combination of sand and dry cement that would harden the ground surface, a product recommended by inventor and entrepreneur Art Troutner.[196]

It didn't take long to see that Troutner's idea wouldn't hold up under the heavy use the Greenbelt was put to. The path became asphalt by default, though bumps caused by tree roots continue to be a problem for cyclists and an expensive repair issue for the city.[197]

The first path in 1971 was six feet wide, but as use increased the city's standards changed. In 1984, the pathway became 10 feet wide, plus two feet clearance on either side of the path, with 14 feet required at underpasses and locations of heavy traffic.[198]

Today the standard is 12 feet, and no six-foot widths remain.[199]

Burns long held out hope to one day convert the Greenbelt to a soft walking material, one that would be beneficial for walkers and the river. The bikes, he said, can move elsewhere.[200]

The issue of the setback took a long time to go away. It was not an easy concept to sell in some circles. The idea of prohibiting buildings within a certain distance from the river was as new to Boise as was the Greenbelt itself, and this was a lot of new ideas to throw at a small, conservative population. While some in the city government, including Stan Burns and John Chapman, wanted a setback three or four hundred feet wide, many property owners, including Morrison

---

195 Nancy Donald interview with Troy Reeves, Boise, Idaho; July 8, 1998.

196 Paul Philbrook, email, January, 20, 2001.

197 Pete Zimowsky, "Tree roots are a real problem on the Greenbelt," *The Idaho Statesman*, Nov. 27, 2005.

198 *Greenbelt Resource Book.*

199 Philbrook e-mail.

200 Burns interview.

Knudsen Corp., which owned a great deal of riverfront property in the then-undeveloped ParkCenter area, resisted the idea altogether.

"They just couldn't see it was going to help them at all, though now they're very happy, I think, that the Greenbelt exists and they can see what we were suggesting was great for them as well," said Chapman in 1998. "One of my disappointments is that that regulation was not adopted initially to give us three or four hundred feet from the river. That's the way it should have been done. That would have been wonderful for the next thousand years. But it's a time past. Politics always enters into these things."[201]

"I've always held very strongly, I still do, that the waterways are public," said Kathleen Day, who served on the Greenbelt Committee in 1974 and agreed with Burns that the setback should have been bigger. She also wanted to prevent having the river lined with private beaches – so many "mini-Malibus." Though the committee met with resistance from some in the business community on these issues, the members decided "we were just going to pursue it and keep after it until it became a reality," Day said. "We were not intimidated, but were disappointed," she said, that the "business community couldn't see the long-range value of not building on the river."[202]

Eventually, Bowen and the majority of park board members settled on a recommendation to make the setback 100 feet.[203] After much debate, the Planning and Zoning Commission sent that recommendation to the city council.

With the matter before the council in 1968, Bill Onweiler found himself positioned to broker a deal. He had already predicted the Greenbelt could be worth more than the urban renewal of the downtown.[204] Nonetheless, the city administration, including Mayor

---

201 Chapman interview.

202 Kathleen Day interview by Troy Reeves, by telephone, Madison, Wisc.; September 19, 1998.

203 Bowen interview.

204 Onweiler document, p. 7.

Jay Amyx, and downtown developers wanted to create a downtown improvement district and a downtown mall. Open space was not high on their agenda, if it was there at all.[205]

Mayor Jay S. Amyx, 1966-74. (Boise City Department of Arts & History)

Three of the five council members were solidly in favor of redevelopment, but the council needed four votes to start renewal. Onweiler's first concern was to preserve the river frontage.

"I told them at that time I thought that if they would help preserve the frontage on the river and build a path between all the present parks and restrict development right on the river, it would create more assessed valuation for the community than the downtown development would. In a back-room arrangement among members of the city council, they agreed to let me pursue the Greenbelt if I gave them their fourth vote for urban renewal. Both worked. What can I say? It was my first trade in politics."[206]

The Greenbelt advocates also got help from Parks Director Bowen and City Planning Director Nelson. The two city officials began to feed Onweiler's expressed predilection with a steady stream of articles and documents on the benefits of open space. They also

---

205 Onwiler document, p. 4.
206 Ibid.

reminded Onweiler how easy it would be to connect the city's existing riverside parks.

Nelson left his city job in 1968, shortly after the Greenbelt concept was approved, to form his own consulting company. The city council promptly hired Arlo Nelson and Associates, later Planning and Research/West, to design and plan the Greenbelt.[207] That same year, he presented to the city and council a panoramic eight-feet by three-feet map of lakes, amphitheaters, footbridges, and playgrounds. A "recreational paradise," that captured the public's imagination.[208] When Onweiler asked Nelson why he had colored the Greenbelt red, Nelson said: "Yes, I know. But you sure can see it."[209]

With Onweiler and Sherman Perry working behind the scenes, the city council went along with the Greenbelt and the setback concept, but the majority of the council did not think Boise landowners would sit still for 100 feet, let alone the 300 to 400 that Chapman, Burns and others wanted. The first setback was established at 50 feet from the 6,500 cfs line or 20 feet from an existing Greenbelt boundary.

The 1968 guidelines stated that buildings (residences and light office) might be "reasonably compatible" if they were separated from the Greenbelt by an adequate buffer zone. The council also banned billboards, tree-cutting and overhead utility lines. The public would have "in perpetuity, unrestricted access to the river and to the special and unique forms of recreation it provides."[210]

The first actual Greenbelt ordinance came in 1971. It was part of the city's zoning law and it included the setback requirement established earlier. In 1978, the ordinance was amended to set the construction limit at 70 feet from the 6,500 cfs mark or five feet from the boundary of all dedications or easements granted to Boise City for Greenbelt purposes in excess of 65 feet.

---

207 Stacy, *When the River Rises*, p.74.
208 Bowen interview.
209 Onweiler document, p. 4.
210 Stacy, *When the River Rises*, pp. 74-75.

Among other things, the 50-foot width effectively eliminated equestrians from the pathway.

"The developers and the owners and so forth who wanted more and more land kept pushing, and finally the city council agreed to let the setback come much closer than it ever should have," said Stan Burns. "The politicians chickened out."[211]

But Keith Gilmore, also an original Greenbelt Committee member, said it is important to look at the decision from the perspective of the times. "Fifty feet really isn't very much, but at that time, to try to tell someone, 'Well, you can't develop along the river,' especially in Idaho, and especially probably in Southwest Idaho, it was sort of a tough thing for people to swallow."[212]

"That (setback) was a very, very controversial thing," said Ken Pursley. "Landowners were extremely skeptical of it. They didn't see the value of a Greenbelt to the development of property. They saw it only as a negative, as a restriction on what they could do. It was a very long, hard fight to get that done. But that was the key to preserving the land until it could be acquired. And it was the key to getting donations of land. Some of the landowners then ended up donating the 50 feet because it was encumbered by a setback anyway."

The setback quickly became a way for the city to acquire property without having to buy it, said Pursley. "Once the setback ordinance was in, they were more than willing in most cases to give us the 50 feet. That way they didn't have to manage or maintain it. It was going to be a setback anyway so they couldn't use it. And (developers) ended up getting credit for it in terms of doing a good project."[213]

---

211 Burns interview.

212 Keith Gilmore interview with Troy Reeves, Boise, Idaho; July 15, 1998.

213 Pursley interview.

Before long, said Morgan Masner, the first chair of the original
Greenbelt Committee in 1969, there were more land donations than
the city could handle.[214]

"We did what we could," said Earl Reynolds. "We wish we had a
quarter-mile strip through the city, but we started when it was already
developed, so that wasn't realistic. Ours is still far more natural than
the River Walk in San Antonio is, a much prettier stream. Given
where we were starting, we did very well."[215]

The important thing, said Pursley, was that the council had the
courage to put the setback ordinance on the books and enforce it, even
if they "weren't out front on it."[216]

In the 1970s, the International Dunes Motel and other property
owners would test that courage in court.

In 1966, the city purchased its first piece of Greenbelt property
when the Taubman Corporation donated 0.43 acres on the north
side of the river, east of Americana Boulevard, between the
Quinn building and the river. Two other small donations followed the
next year. The cover of the Boise Parks & Recreation Department
1967 Annual Report featured a cartoon of a belt hatching from an egg.
The caption read: "Boise River Greenbelt Project is Born."[217]

But the Greenbelt pioneers knew it would take more than a few
parcels of donated land and a setback ordinance. If this idea was to
become something people could actually walk on, the Greenbelt
would require greenbacks. Onweiler reasoned that if the city
government purchased some Greenbelt land on its own, Boise would
not be able to turn back. He and Sherman Perry began the search.

---

214 Masner interview.

215 Reynolds interview.

216 Pursley interview.

217 Stacy, *When the River Rises*, p.74.

"Bill Onweiler was always ready to look for money, to buttonhole council members looking for money," said Morgan Masner.[218]

Since there was little park-acquisition money to be had in Boise, during the summer of 1968, Onweiler went where the money was – Washington, D.C. It wasn't a direct flight, however.

At the time, Onweiler had just declined a trip to Boston to attend an Association of American Cities meeting when he realized how close the conference would be to the capitol. He reversed his decision not to attend the AAC meeting, and suggested to Sherman Perry they take a small detour on the way to Boston and see if they could shake a little money loose. With Perry on board, Onweiler called Idaho's Republican Senator Len Jordan and set up an appointment.[219]

---

218 Masner interview.
219 Onweiler document, p. 17.

*The 1968 greenbelt meeting of Bill Onweiler (left), Sherman Perry
(center) and Senator Frank Church. Later, Church was able to tap
two different federal funds for $100,000. The allocation allowed the
city of Boise to purchase 12 acres of riverfront property during the
early stages of the Greenbelt's development. (Frank Church papers,
Boise State University special collections)*

In Jordan's office, the three of them chatted for nearly 45 minutes before Jordan finally said, "What the hell are you guys here for?" Perry told the senator about the Greenbelt idea and that they wanted to purchase a little property to ensure that the city didn't forget its commitment. Jordan expressed interest, but told them: "If you really want to get some money, I will call Frank (Church). He will take care of you. That is in his bailiwick." The two Republicans reluctantly trudged down the hall to see Idaho's Democratic senator.

Church listened to their sales pitch, looked at the map the city had created and told them he had had a similar idea years earlier, before he got into politics. Church said that at the time he thought if he could get his service club involved, others would follow and together they "could build a path all the way through. I got elected instead."[220]

Onweiler and Perry told Church that for about $100,000 they thought the city could buy a piece of what was then the Links School of Business property that ran along the river near 9th Street and Royal Boulevard. Church promised to get back to them within two weeks. A week later Church's office called Onweiler and said the senator had found the money, and the city should be prepared to spend it. Onweiler only recalled that Church had found the money in "the Bureau of, well, some damn thing or another,"[221] but the senator had actually tapped two different funds. Half came from the Interior Department's contingency funds and half from Idaho's regularly apportioned share of the Land and Water Conservation Fund, established by Congress to develop outdoor park and recreation areas. Church had been the floor manager when Congress passed the new Land and Water Conservation bill, which is why Jordan had sent Onweiler and Perry to him in the first place.

The press release that announced the grants stated that the money would be used to purchase 12 acres along the river, and that this was the first step in Boise's effort to acquire 300 riverfront acres for a

220 Onweiler interview.
221 Ibid.

project that would eventually "include swimming and boating facilities, riding and hiking trails, a golf course, picnic areas and playing fields."[222] Onweiler describes this funding, the first money actually allocated to buy land for the Greenbelt, as what the city needed to "cross the Rubicon."[223]

Onweiler and Perry then got the city to pencil some matching funds for the Greenbelt – $15,000 or $20,000, Onweiler recalled – into the proposed city budget. It was the third year of the Greenbelt as a city concept and the first time the city had budgeted any real money. When the entire city budget went to the required public hearing, the reaction caught the city officials by surprise. What was normally a pro forma and sparsely attended meeting drew a substantial audience. "There were so many anti-government people that we could not get them into City Hall," Onweiler said.[224]

While the Greenbelt was not the target of the public's ire, the crowd at the hearing was an indication of how Boiseans felt about taxes and government spending in general. After all, Idaho voters hadn't approved a sales tax until two years before, in 1966.[225] If anyone in City Hall had thoughts of a public willing to open its wallet to pay for the Greenbelt, the response at the budget hearing scotched that idea. It was, said Onweiler, the first rumblings of the tax revolt that would roar into life in 1978 as the Idaho's One Percent tax limitation initiative.[226]

With the old city hall building on the southwest corner of 6th and Bannock streets too small to hold those who wanted to attend the meeting, Mayor Jay Amyx marched the whole crowd, public and council alike, across Jefferson Street to the Idaho Statehouse, up to the

---

222 Sen. Frank Church press release, dated August 1968, from Boise State University Library, Special Collections.

223 Onweiler document, p. 16.

224 Onweiler interview.

225 Randy Stapilus, *Paradox Politics*, p. 255.

226 Onweiler interview.

third floor and held the meeting in the State Senate chambers. Amyx sat in the Senate president's chair and ran the hearing.

Bill Onweiler: "He commenced to preach on each item in the budget. They would ask him questions, and he would have good answers. It went until about 11:30. We wished it was over with, because he was a preacher by nature. Finally, some guy who read the damn budget got up and said, 'Well, there is an item in here,' I'm going to say 15 maybe it was 20, thousand, 'for a greenbelt through Boise. What is that? Why do we need it?'

"And Amyx stopped, and he looked at me. And I am about half asleep. He said, 'I don't really understand that very well, but Councilman Onweller will explain it to you.' He'd never been able to pronounce my name. And I thought for a minute, Now, he did say me, didn't he? I don't have the vaguest idea what I told the guy, but he was happy. I gave a five-minute speech, and I don't know where the hell it came from. But we survived it (and the budget passed)."[227]

It wasn't the last debate. For while the Greenbelt concept stayed popular with most Boiseans, there were always vocal minorities who nipped at the city's heels at almost every step. If it wasn't tax-protesters, it was landowners and developers.

"We even had one public hearing where they threw tomatoes," recalled John Chapman. "It's hard to believe now that these people would feel so strongly against the Greenbelt concept, because I think now everyone has accepted it as being a wonderful thing for Boise. In those days it wasn't easy to convince some people that the Greenbelt was best for them, but it certainly has turned out that way."[228]

One of the prevailing schools of thought at the time was, "I didn't have anyone fixing up a football field for me when I was growing up,

227 Ibid.
228 Chapman interview.

why should we spend taxpayers' money to do one now?" said committee member Orland Mayer.[229]

Fortunately, the protesters were a minority. Despite the still-deplorable state of the Boise River, the Greenbelt idea – parks and public access along its entire length – had caught on with most Boise residents. "We hoped that the public could be brought out to see what an asset we had in the river and that they would use the river, not turn their backs on it," said Parks Commissioner Alice Dieter.[230]

The commissioners' dream came true, and for the next decade private citizens and a variety of government agencies undertook a series of campaigns, large and small, to turn the river from detriment to asset. People from the private sector, service clubs, scouting groups, environmental groups, local corporations and myriad individuals rediscovered the river's recreational possibilities and staged clean-up programs.[231]

Onweiler became intensely involved in the rehabilitation process, and as a result towed his children into a long list of places they would rather not have gone. In 1987, he wrote a letter to his children in which he apologized for both dragging them along as he explored the future Greenbelt and spending so much time away while he worked to make the pathway a reality.

"We ate with bugs in the Old Soldiers Home area, crawled over barbed wire buried back of a business at the Fairview Bridge and were run off by shotgun from the Farmers Canal near the river," he wrote.[232]

---

229 Mayer interview.

230 Dieter interview.

231 Stacy, *When the River Rises*, p.74.

232 Rodgers, *The Idaho Statesman*. Greenbelt special section, p.4.

*Greenbelt pioneer Bill Onweiler
in 1972. (Idaho Statesman
Archives, BSU Special
Collections)*

The parks staff had it no easier. Even after a right-of-way was acquired, workers had to bushwhack their way through weeds and thorns to install the sprinkler system and make other improvements. Near American Boulevard, behind where the Quinn Center building was located, was "a nasty stretch of river, a no-man's land" that served as a dumping area for construction-trades businesses, said Jerry Tracy. "It was a real challenge to get to the river."[233] From the path, between the Americana and Fairview bridges, old sheet metal, wire and rebar were visible for years through the weeds.

Another difficult spot early on was the three-acre Goodman Oil property that backed up to the river from Fletcher and 29th streets. It's now a vacant lot, but it once was the site of one of the largest businesses in the Northwest. When the Greenbelt began to become a reality, the land closest to the river, about 75 feet deep from the Goodman warehouse to the river, was a disposal area "hip deep in wire and trash."[234]

The bike path by then had been completed on both the west side and east side of the Goodman property and the adjacent land owned

233 Tracy interview, Proctor.

234 Kathleen Kreller, "Boise oil property may be a diamond in the rough," *Idaho Statesman*, March 31, 2008.

by the Union Pacific Railroad. After much negotiation, the city got permission to go through the Union Pacific property. "Mr. Goodman, however, was very much against the Greenbelt," said committee member Nelson Miller. Miller and Bill Onweiler separately lobbied owner Roy Goodman, a big-game hunter whom Onweiler describes as "a grizzled little man in peg pants and lace-up boots,"[235] in an attempt to persuade him to grant an easement. "He would generally, sometimes quite vociferously, tell me to leave,"[236] Miller said. Onweiler got the same treatment, despite the fact that Goodman and Onweiler's father had been on friendly terms.[237]

Alice Dieter attributes at least some of that attitude, and others like it, to the political climate at the time. Not only did Goodman fear damage to his oil tanks, "we were just coming out of the McCarthy period in this town. Metro government was communism, and planning was suspect," she said.[238]

The solution to this dilemma came, Miller says, purely by accident. When Parks Director Jack Cooper let the contract to pave the path through the Union Pacific property, he had an alternate bid prepared with the same contractor to continue through the Goodman property, just in case Miller's negotiations were successful. "Very, very early one morning the contractor made a big mistake and just punched that trail right through Goodman's property and paved it," Miller recalled. After a period of arguing and negotiation, the city agreed to erect a chain-link fence to protect Goodman's oil tanks and the rest of his property from the Greenbelt. "But once the path was there, it didn't go away. People used it, and it stayed," Miller said.[239]

Cooper himself has a different, and less dramatic, memory of the Goodman property. "The contractor did pave a few feet over the

---

235 Onweiler document, p. 26.
236 Miller interview.
237 Onweiler document, p. 26.
238 Dieter interview.
239 Miller interview.

property line but not the entire width of the parcel," Cooper said. "Barricades were placed at each side of the Goodman parcel to prevent access."[240]

The development of this section was further complicated by disagreements over changed property lines on the land the river had added over the years. The "Goodman section" was eventually paved, but was done primarily off the Goodman property, when a gabion wall (a wall made of cylindrical shapes) was built along that stretch, he said.[241] The Goodman buildings have since been razed and the wall replaced by a simple chain-link fence.

The second front of the Greenbelt offensive was the effort to get the river itself clean enough to make the Greenbelt idea worth pursuing. This effort began in the mid-1960s and continues to the present day. The first important step was the construction of the Boise sewage treatment plant in 1950. It was only then that "Boise had stopped pouring its raw sewage into the river."[242] But many food-processing plants and private homes still used the river as a sewer.

"The city put in a sewer, and still we couldn't get them to hook up," said Bill Onweiler. "They didn't want to pay the fee."[243]

The city's response was to take an aerial, heat-sensitive photo of the river, similar to the technique used in Vietnam to track enemy soldiers. The photo revealed where all the sewer pipes entered the river.

"And the threat went out," said Onweiler, "that we knew where they were, and the owners were going to stop dumping or we were going to drive a plug into every pipe. And they stopped. And that is why you can ride a raft along that river. Otherwise, there were turds all the way. It was just awful."

---

240 Cooper written comments, p. 2.
241 Ibid.
242 Stacy, *When the River Rises*, p.70.
243 Onweiler interview.

On the larger national stage, the ecology movement of the 1970s continued to have an impact on national politics, and by extension on Idaho. As part of the 1972 Clean Water Act, the Corps of Engineers was given the funds and authority to assist communities nationwide as they sought alternatives to dumping wastes into rivers.

The governments of Ada and downstream neighbor Canyon counties joined forces with the Corps and used mostly federal money to tackle the Boise River's water quality problem. It was, historian Stacy noted, "one of the first times that local and federal agencies collaborated during the early planning stages to deal with such a complex problem in a comprehensive way."[244]

In 1966, researchers found the Boise River contained 63,000 to 83,000 bacteria per millimeter. In 1973, tested in the same place, downstream from the city, the water tested at 2,800 to 11,000 bacteria per milliliter. Mayflies and stoneflies, gone for decades, returned and with them came the fish.[245]

---

244 Stacy, p. 77.
245 Nate Johnson, *Boise Weekly*, "A River Runs Through It"

5 The Greenbelt Committee

"I do not think that I have ever done anything in my life that I am more proud of."

– Morgan Masner, chair of original Greenbelt Committee

For five years after the Atkinson Report and for three years after the first Greenbelt ordinance, the Greenbelt was managed internally by the Boise Parks & Recreation Department in much the same manner as it ran Julia Davis and Ann Morrison parks. By 1969, Park Commissioner Alice Dieter saw the need for a separate committee to deal solely with the unique requirements of the Greenbelt, particularly the sometimes-sticky issue of land acquisition. "I felt it would be politically disastrous to try and sell the purchase of property in the same (Park) budget for two different purposes," she said.

Her idea was that the Greenbelt Committee would be responsible to the park board but would have a separate budget approved by the city council.[246]

In April 1969, the park board approved the idea. That summer, the Planning and Zoning Commission recommended to the city council that it create a separate board to oversee the Greenbelt. The council

---

246 Dieter interview.

agreed and created the Boise River Greenbelt Committee on August 25, 1969, as part of the mayor's office. In its first incarnation, the committee was an advisory board composed of city and county residents who volunteered to assist the park board and city council. It was an independent body but worked with both the city council and park board. The latter retained responsibility for property acquisition and development.[247]

In 1970, the city's organizational chart was restructured. While it remained an advisory board, the committee became independent of the park board and reported solely to the mayor and council, a move that markedly increased its ability to influence the Greenbelt's development.[248] In 1986, Mayor Dirk Kempthorne reduced that influence when he moved the committee out of his office and had it report to the city's Planning and Zoning Commission.

The committee, however, remained the keystone of the city's recreational architecture. In 1992, the Boise River Greenbelt Committee became the Boise River Greenbelt and Pathways Committee when it undertook the responsibility to review and promote trails and pathways throughout the city. This trail system eventually included Boise's Ridge to Rivers Pathway Plan, a program created to connect the trails in the Boise Foothills through downtown Boise to the urban Greenbelt path system.

The first Greenbelt Committee, appointed by Mayor Jay Amyx, was confirmed by the city council on September 22, 1969.[249] Members of that first group were two-year appointees Keith Gilmore, Edna Adams and County Commissioner Jack Barney (all representing Ada County), three-year appointments Stanley Burns (representing the parks board), Earl Reynolds, Jr., (Planning and Zoning Commission) and Morgan Masner (Boise Chamber of Commerce), and four-year appointments Orland Mayer (parks board), Gay Davis and Larry

---

247 Gordon Bowen written comments.

248 *Greenbelt Resource Book.*

249 City document, mayor's letter to City Council.

Jackson. Bill Onweiler was the city council liaison and Dick Hammond was secretary. Amyx named Masner interim chair.[250] Gordon Bowen remained as parks director and functioned as the committee's staff advisor.

Larry Jackson, circa 1974 (Boise State University Special Collections)

Onweiler singles out Masner as "another unsung hero of the Greenbelt," someone who cared deeply and worked hard to make it a reality.[251] Masner was employed at the time by Ore-Ida Foods, which had recently moved to Boise. As a company, Ore-Ida encouraged its employees to be involved in local affairs and Masner, a native Boisean, knew about the Greenbelt and had worked on the Chamber of Commerce's parks committee. One of the projects he tackled with the committee was to help clean up the Boise River banks.

Mayor Amyx took note of the chamber's project and promptly offered Masner the chairmanship of the first Greenbelt Committee. "I said fine, but I don't want to be the guy who appoints the members," said Masner. Amyx reassured him it was the mayor's job to make the appointments. Looking back, Masner is thankful for the opportunity. "I do not think that I have ever done anything in my life that I am more proud of. It is a wonderful amenity to the city."

---

250 Bowen interview.
251 Onweiler document, p. 23.

Masner was later elected to the Eagle City Council and voted to extend the Greenbelt through Eagle.[252]

When Mayor Amyx looked around for people to fill in the committee, he did it the same way he made many of his personnel decisions: Find someone passionate about something and put him or her in a position to tackle that project. Stanley Burns was convinced that is how he ended up on the Greenbelt Committee.[253]

As a citizen, Burns got Amyx's attention by bringing up the idea of river restoration and preservation at city council meetings. Burns said Amyx appointed him to the parks board "thinking that way he could give me something to do besides come to city council meetings."

Not everyone on the committee was so well versed. Orland Mayer, then a recently retired Idaho Power engineer, said his first reaction to his appointment was: "I don't know what this is all about." In time, "we all learned as a group, you might say. So it became very much a cooperative thing. We all had to get the opinions of the other committee members when things like land acquisition came up."[254]

What the committee members did have, though, was expertise in a wide variety of professions that could be brought to bear on the development process. Glen Cline was an architect. John Chapman was an attorney who knew property law. Gay Davis could appeal to both women's groups and business owners. Jack Barney was an Ada County commissioner, and many times city funds came through the county. Barney's position also gave him serious clout when he talked to developers who knew he was one of three votes on the board of county commissioners. Mayer and Reynolds were engineers. Masner was a well-connected businessman. Burns was a respected community activist. Bill Onweiler had a nose for money, both within the city and later as a member of the Idaho Legislature.

---

252 Masner interview.
253 Burns interview.
254 Masner interview.

Subsequent members also brought their individual portfolios with them to the committee. Art Troutner had a mountain of influence as a very successful businessman and inventor. Ken Pursley was an attorney and brought an independent voice to the process. Dick d'Easum was a historian and used the lessons of history to avoid repeating the mistakes of the past. Jan Evans was a banker who used the connections he built at First Security to help create the J.D. Evans Golf Course, now the Warm Springs Golf Course, as an anchor to the east end of the Greenbelt.

One of the first requests Masner made in his new position as Greenbelt Committee chair was for a half-time person to run down leads on property, look for ways to finance land and oversee the many tree donations. At the time, as a way to save the city money, people donated their trees to the Greenbelt. The city would then dig them up and plant them near the river.

Masner told Amyx the person he wanted was Bill Onweiler. Amyx agreed, and even though he was still on the city council, Onweiler became the first Greenbelt coordinator, a position that, like the committee itself, was made part of the mayor's office.[255]

"It was a very humble beginning," said Masner. "We had no budget. We only had people with a great love for the community and the desire to do something that would be long lasting and would help clean up our beautiful river."

Onweiler was convinced Amyx disliked the Greenbelt plan, that the mayor felt it interfered with the growth plan he had in mind for Boise.[256] "Jay Amyx was the mayor at the time," Elizabeth Van Zonneveld said, "and he wasn't really in favor of the Greenbelt. Maybe he put it (coordinator's position) in his own office in order to keep an eye on it. But it happened before I got there, so I really don't know that."[257] Masner begs to differ: "Mayor Amyx was absolutely

255 Ibid.

256 Onweiler interview.

257 Van Zonneveld interview.

great to work with. If we wanted him to go to the council and ask for this or that or money or purchases, he had the vision and the determination to do it."[258]

For the next 20 years, Boise's city officials and Greenbelt Committee members would need all the vision and determination they could muster as the Greenbelt's popularity became both its greatest strength and its greatest liability.

T he Greenbelt Committee also had internal issues. Gordon Bowen resigned in 1977, and Jack Cooper became director of Boise Parks & Recreation Department the next year. With that transition came a new approach to the way the Greenbelt Committee operated.

Early on, the committee worked with great autonomy. It set its own agenda and did most of its own research. In those years, the members' primary jobs were to sell the Greenbelt concept, acquire property and plan for Greenbelt expansion. For the first several years of the committee's life, there was no staff help at all. Cooper came to the Parks Department in 1978, during a period of tremendous growth in Boise. The city and the government were becoming more sophisticated. Under Cooper, the Parks Department followed suit. The professional parks staff began to do the research and set the committee's agenda.

One consequence of this maturation process was that many committee members felt they became more part of the bureaucracy and less personally involved.

"That made us all just kind of participating 'yes' people," said Nancy Donald, who served from 1974-1997. "In the beginning, we did a lot more on-site trips. We probably went on two or three tours a year. I liked it better that way. Once it became staff oriented, the staff

---

258 Masner interview.

would give their input and guide us along based more on their feelings than on how we all felt."²⁵⁹

Jack Cooper doesn't buy this assessment completely. "The committee conducted project-specific site inspections," he said, and added, "I do not recall members of the time being the kind of personalities that would be called 'yes people.' In fact, Nancy was clearly outspoken and emphatically supported the Greenbelt from the users' point of view."²⁶⁰

City Parks Director Jack Cooper, in 1979. (Idaho Statesman)

The Greenbelt Committee may have become more detached, but they were no less busy. As the popularity of the Greenbelt grew, the land along the river became more valuable. Requests for building permits increased, and the proposals the committee faced for developments along the river became larger and often more difficult. The work flow changed. The parks staff submitted information to the Boise Planning and Zoning Commission and the Greenbelt Committee rather than the committee members doing the legwork and research on their own.

---

259 Nancy Donald interview with Troy Reeves, Boise, Idaho; July 8, 1998.
260 Cooper, written comments, p. 3].

In the 1980s, the committee focused less on advocacy and more on project reviews to ensure builders maintained the setback and met the other Greenbelt requirements. This shift required committee members to anticipate how individual developments would unfold and what problems they would present to the Greenbelt for years into the future. These were different skills than selling the Greenbelt concept, and some feel the committee faltered on occasion as it carried out its new mission.

It may have. Several past Greenbelt Committee members now look back and with twenty-twenty hindsight see votes they wish had gone differently. Nevertheless, despite the fact they often operated under great pressure from developers large and small and only had the power to make recommendations to the Planning and Zoning Commission, the volunteers who filled the committee's seats over the years did a remarkable job of preserving the original intent of the Greenbelt pioneers. It's not easy in a small city like Boise to say no as often as they said it. The committee members and the applicants usually knew each other, and there were powerful property owners looking over the members' shoulders, pushing to get as close to the river as possible.

Every townhouse building and office building had to be checked on. Every land exchange, large or small, dealings with the Ada County Highway District, flood repairs and even helicopters came before the committee.

A townhouse project along Walnut Street had a sprinkler system and plantings that encroached on the setback.

The Alscott Foundation wanted to use the roof of its building, located near the river in the ParkCenter area, as a helipad "because it would greatly contribute to the efficiency of Alscott's business and foundation operations." Despite Alscott's close ties to the influential

Albertsons grocery chain – CEO Joe Scott is an Albertson grandson – the committee recommended the city decline the request.[261]

When construction bids came in too high – as they did for the Main Street tunnel in December 1981[262] – the jobs had to be broken down and re-bid separately.

When a new alignment for Pioneer Walk, between downtown and the Greenbelt, was proposed, the committee reviewed plans and suggested changes to reduce the canyon effect of walking between large buildings. The volunteers even had to arbitrate conflicts between pedestrians, equestrians and bicyclists.

In the 1990s, the committee found itself in long, multi-meeting discussions with restaurant owners who wanted to build their decks as close to the river as possible, including proposals to build them out over the Greenbelt.

Every river-land annexation was reviewed to see the Greenbelt was kept in mind. Every footbridge, every restaurant parking lot, the Boise River Festival, the installation of telephones along the Greenbelt, raptor wintering areas, water well structures near the river, property acquisition from stubborn owners, whether permitted buildings were properly screened from the path, Fire Department access through property, trail alignment through Military Reserve Park, speed limit on the Greenbelt (10 mph on approaches and 15 mph on the Greenbelt itself)[263] and the ongoing discussions with Boise State University about its expansion plans all went under the committee's microscope. Underpass construction, flooding, roots that buckled the path, the quality of materials used by developers for retainers around trees, whether the sponsoring companies should get their names on the Greenbelt mileage markers (the committee decided companies were getting enough publicity for donating that they didn't have to get

---

261 Greenbelt Committee minutes, February 1, 1996.

262 Ibid, May 10, 1984.

263 Ibid, March 4, 1993.

names on bollards), when and where to permit alcohol, what restrictions to put on dogs, how to preserve the Oregon Trail ruts that run through Southeast Boise – it all came before the Greenbelt Committee.

Fortunately, committee members tended to be long-term. Ten years was not an uncommon length of service, which helped preserve the committee's institutional memory and high standards.

"These were exciting times with a wide variety of projects and developer techniques being presented to the committee. The committee members performed a remarkable service to the community considering the mounting pressures," said former Parks Department director Jack Cooper.[264]

---

264 Cooper, written comments, p.3.

6 Bumps in the Path

"Everybody wanted a variance"

– *Bert Cleaveland, Greenbelt Committee member*

The Greenbelt's first run of luck lasted a good long time given the enormity of the project and the number of lives and livelihoods on which it had an impact. Though the cards turned a little sour later on, in the late 1960s and early 1970s, volunteers launched cleanup projects on a regular basis, federal clean-water and flood-protection laws made tax money available to clean up the river and its banks, and the Boise Parks Department continued to acquire property.

Greenbelt Committee members were often in the forefront of the cleanup campaigns. Bill Onweiler dragged his children into some of the most inhospitable stretches on the riverbank. The William Onweiler Pathway now starts at Capitol Boulevard on the north side of the river and extends a mile west toward Shoreline Park. John Chapman, who later chaired the committee, organized a weekend cleanup of a short but particularly difficult stretch from the Clements cement plant (now Shoreline Park) nearly to the Americana Bridge.

"It was the ugliest goddamn mess you ever saw in your life,"
recalled Onweiler of the Chapman effort. "They cleaned it up and
planted it. They got tractors in there and just tore the hell out of it. You
probably couldn't do that today."[265]

"We particularly were worried that the Boise River would become
like the Portneuf River in Pocatello, just a cement sewer through the
city," said John Chapman. "We wanted to avoid that and preserve the
fisheries and the wildlife as well as the public access to the river."[266]

Riparian and fish habitat were not big issues at the time, said
Morgan Masner. "We figured out there was some wildlife down there,
and there were some fish down there, but they were kind of on their
own as far as we were concerned," he laughed. "But we didn't like the
environment that had developed down there. It was a place to dump
refuse, a seedy, crummy-looking place."[267]

Efforts like Chapman's made an impression on Boise public
opinion. "I think a lot of people looked at that and said it could be
done," Onweiler said. It also helped the budget process, he noted,
because people saw what the entire river could look like and were less
inclined to throw tomatoes and other produce at city budget writers
who included Greenbelt money.[268]

In 1970, an accident tragically accelerated the cleanup effort. A 12-
year-old boy drowned when a metal pipe in the river, that had been
part of an irrigation diversion structure, snagged his inner tube. In
1971, assisted by a low-water year, the city undertook a massive civic
cleanup effort sponsored by Boise's American Legion post and the
Idaho Department of Lands and coordinated by the chamber of
commerce. Groups that included students from Boise High School and
Boise State College, the Idaho National Guard and the Seabees,
Boise-based corporations and hundreds of individuals scoured the

265 Onweiler interview.
266 Chapman interview.
267 Masner interview.
268 Onweiler interview.

riverbed for debris and even repaired and replaced old diversion structures. The next year a volunteer effort rebuilt the diversion dam below Ann Morrison Park. The Sierra Club and Jaycees joined forces with the Army Reserves to haul off huge concrete slabs, remnants from past flood-control efforts. One group tracked and recorded the remaining pollution sources. Cleanup efforts continue to this day and are important entries on many civic groups' annual public service calendars.[269]

While volunteer labor was the currency that paid for most of this work, the city still needed greenbacks to buy portions of the Greenbelt that weren't donated. After Senator Frank Church obtained federal Land and Water Conservation Funds in 1968, the city became a regular applicant for that money. It also made good use of the 1967 Army Corps of Engineers report titled *Flood Plain Information, Boise Idaho and Vicinity*. Among other things, the report illustrated where the water would flow should a 100-year flood occur. This information helped the city strengthen its argument in favor of a setback, and in 1970 the city council added language to the Greenbelt guidelines that stated the Greenbelt could use "delineated flood-plain properties on which permanent construction is necessarily restricted."[270]

The Boise Greenbelt got another helping hand from Washington when the federal government decided it was time to clean up the nation's waterways. In 1972, Congress passed the Clean Water Act, which helped the city crack down on people and companies that dumped directly into the river – to the tune of $30 million over 20 years. The same law helped chase the meatpacking plants out of the city.[271] Congress also gave the Corps of Engineers the funds and authority to provide technical assistance to local governments to help them find alternatives to dumping wastes into rivers. Public agencies in Ada and Canyon counties began their innovative collaboration with

---

269 Stacy, p.78.

270 Ibid, p.75.

271 Timothy Noah, *Wall Street Journal*, April 22, 1994.

the Corps, using the Corps' money, of course, to improve the water quality of the Boise River. That work led to a second wastewater treatment plant in Boise and actions to reduce pollution from feedlots, meatpacking plants, irrigation-return flow, urban storm runoff and other sources.[272] The Corps became, for all intents and purposes, the city's river engineers. Flood-control decisions of all kinds, including riverside developments that had big impacts on the Greenbelt, were passed to the Corp. If the Engineers approved it, the city approved it.

As the river's popularity increased, the Greenbelt's momentum began to build on its own success.

The water became cleaner and more people came back to it. The more people came back to it, the easier it was to get support for cleanup efforts and to keep it clean. Instead of recreational floaters getting out early to avoid the downstream pollution, the tubing run – the stretch of river people used to float on rafts and inner tubes – was extended from what would become Barber Park in 1972 all the way to Ann Morrison Park. Game fish – trout and whitefish – replaced trash fish such as suckers and carp, which in turn brought fishermen and eagles back to the river.[273]

Another stroke of good fortune came when the state of Idaho agreed to give the city 52 acres east of town for the city's first municipal golf course. The land had been reclaimed from the river with labor "donated" by inmates and had become part of the state penitentiary.[274] Warden Louis Clapp had used the property for many years as a prison farm. It was Clapp's idea, said his daughter Marilyn, that prisoners should learn "a trade to help pay the costs of incarceration."[275]

---

272 Stacy, p. 77.

273 Noah, *Wall Street Journal.*

274 Tim Woodward, "Warden's Daughter Recalls Life in Old Pen," *The Idaho Statesman,* Feb. 4, 2001, p. 1B.

275 Onweiler interview.

Of course, these 52 acres were not gifted to the city out of the blue. Back in 1966, city planner Arlo Nelson had recommended to the parks board that the city obtain land east of the city for a golf course as part of the Greenbelt acquisition program. Not only would the course enhance the Greenbelt, Nelson reasoned, but because the land was in the floodplain, the city might also be able to use Land and Conservation funds to buy it.[276] The state later sold the city another 42 acres.[277] Warden Clapp, who went on to become Idaho secretary of state, supported the idea. In fact, Bill Onweiler said it was Clapp's idea from the beginning that the reclaimed land would be perfect for golf.[278]

Onweiler, by then a member of the Idaho Legislature, convinced fellow lawmakers Ferd Koch, former president of the Boise City Council, and Emery Hedlund of St. Maries that this was a deal that needed to be done. And he convinced Hedlund, as a representative from outside Boise, he was the man to do it. Hedlund helped push the land transfer through, and Onweiler called it "the best stolen piece of ground in Boise."[279]

Additional land came from the Boise Water Corporation. During negotiations with the city council to retain its lucrative city franchise, the company agreed to make the surface rights of the land above its wells available for a city golf course.[280]

At City Hall, the late Greenbelt Committee member, banker and avid golfer Jan Evans made the golf course his personal crusade. "Jan was a mover and a shaker in the community, and he had a way with people that was just wonderful," said Morgan Masner. "He had vision. He'd been in the community for years and years and was winding down his career at First Security. His idea was, let's put a golf course

---

276 Bowen interview.
277 Philbrook email.
278 Onweiler document, p. 8.
279 Onweiler interview.
280 Onweiler document, p. 16.

on one end of it. That was one of the biggest projects we tackled, and we could never have done that if it had not been for him."

Evans went on to lease the course from the city and run it after he retired from the bank, and for a time it was named after him – the J.D. Evans Golf Course.[281] Now operated by the city, the course is known as the Warm Springs Golf Course.

After the golf course, Boise's land acquisitions became less friendly and more expensive.

Between 1970 and 1977, the city acquired 17 tracts totaling 72 acres.[282] And everyone along those stretches, it seemed, wanted a variance to build into the setback.

"I was really bothered by the people who wanted to build along the Greenbelt," said Bert Cleaveland, who served on the committee in the early to mid-1990s. "In five years, I remember only one group that came in that didn't ask for a variance."

With great foresight, the committee rarely took any action that might have been construed as a precedent, which could then be used to force the city to grant a variance to the setback in the future. As they saw it, their job was to protect the Greenbelt, not enrich landowners.[283]

Boise City also displayed its commitment to obtain Greenbelt property and established the city's serious intent to follow through on its Greenbelt plan.

In 1970, Boise went after two acres owned by the W.E. Clements & Sons Concrete Company. "It was just awful," said John Chapman of the batch plant. "If we had allowed that to continue it would have destroyed the whole beauty of the Greenbelt."[284]

---

281 Masner interview.

282 Stacy, p. 76.

283 Bert Cleaveland interview with Troy Reeves, Boise, Idaho; July 15, 1998.

284 Chapman interview.

Bill Onweiler, an appraiser by profession, assessed the land, but the company refused to sell unless the price was increased dramatically. The city refused and initiated condemnation proceedings. The owners took the city to court. Boise won the case and the land, but the court ordered the city to pay $127,500.[285]

"Boy, did we get pasted in court," said Alice Dieter. "I think it was three times (Onweiler's) appraisal the city had to pay for that condemnation."[286]

But Chapman and others felt it was "a tremendous accomplishment, to acquire the title to the cement plant, then to work with a landscape architect so it would be attractive," Chapman said. "It was a real challenge. It turned out to be one of the best parts of the Greenbelt."

The Clements property was cleaned up and landscaped and in July 1975, became Shoreline Park. Located at 13th and River streets, it was the first dedicated stretch of Greenbelt.

The legal dustup with the International Dunes Motel was another watershed that forced the city government to reassess and reassert its commitment to the Greenbelt.

In 1974, the motel, which became the Shiloh Inn and has since been rebuilt into the Cottonwood Suites, built a swimming pool that encroached into the Greenbelt setback, which was by then a well-established city zoning regulation. Once the pool was built, the motel owners applied for an after-the-fact zoning variance. The city council, sitting as the city's Board of Adjustment, voted thumbs down. The motel appealed to the city council itself, and on April 14, 1974, the council denied it. The motel owners took the city to district court. Among other issues, they argued the setback was unconstitutional.

---

285 Philbrook e-mail.
286 Dieter interview.

The complaint was dismissed,[287] and the owners not only had to move the pool, they had to build Greenbelt access into their parking lot.[288]

Elizabeth Van Zonneveld said the Dunes victory is one of the things she was most proud of as Greenbelt coordinator. "In those days, nobody ever bucked a developer," she said. "Just the idea that someone wanted to put a motel in town made it okay. The motel owners cheated, basically, and expected the building department to go along with it. In the original drawings their swimming pool stuck out into the Greenbelt. We told them it encroached into the setback, so they agreed and moved the pool into a parking lot area between two buildings. Then, lo and behold, when they built the building, they put the swimming pool right out in the original place. They just disregarded us. The city red-tagged it and shut down the construction."

The case boosted the Greenbelt's stock immensely, said Van Zonneveld, "because the city council supported the Greenbelt project instead of the developer. It was a real turning point in the attitudes of the city government."[289]

"Second to actually getting the setback, having the setback ordinance, the legality of it, sustained by a judge was crucial to the development of the rest of the Greenbelt," said Ken Pursley.[290]

Van Zonneveld also cites Jim Quinn's turnabout as one of the important early achievements of which she was part.

"Quinn-Robbins was a construction company with a lot of gravel pits along the side of the river, basically in the heart of town," she said. "They were very much opposed to the public development of the river, and it took lots of meeting and explaining to convince Jim

---

287 Stacy, *When the River Rises*, pp. 78-79.

288 Tracy interview.

289 Van Zonneveld interview.

290 Pursley interview.

Quinn that the land he still owned, after he gave part of it to the city, was going to be much more valuable for business."

Quinn went on to build the successful Quinn Center office building on the remaining land.

"That was a real landmark," said Van Zonneveld. "It was an important change in attitude because that was a very visible company and one whose owners carried a fair amount of weight in the city. Getting them to agree made it obvious to other landowners that it wasn't a bad business decision to do that. People knew Quinn-Robbins wouldn't do anything dumb with their land."[291]

The land Quinn donated is now known at Bernadine Quinn Riverside Park, named after Jim Quinn's mother.

"Many businesses realized that if they had property next to the Greenbelt, that it wasn't theirs to control, even though they might have been using it, because it was in the floodplain or floodway" said Orland Mayer. "They were satisfied to see something come in there that took care of that and more or less made a frontage for their places. And a lot of them, when they built, would have their lawns running right up to the Greenbelt. Without the Greenbelt, it would have just been a mass of weeds and shrubs. They realized the Greenbelt was really a good thing for them as the property owner because they couldn't use that land anyway."[292]

But not every negotiation was so successful. In the next several years, the Greenbelt Committee encountered a number of recalcitrant landowners who could not be convinced that having the Greenbelt run full width through their property was ultimately to their benefit. Chief among them was Boise State University.

Bill Onweiler's political luck began to turn sour in 1969. Like the Greenbelt he helped create, he had been on a roll for a long time

---

291 Van Zonneveld interview.
292 Mayer interview.

before he began to run into opposition. He had for years aggressively, and successfully, promoted the Greenbelt as a member of the city council and the first Greenbelt coordinator. In 1968, he ran for and won a seat in the state house of representatives while he kept his council seat. But Onweiler's single-minded vision and go-go ways began to wear thin, both with his colleagues and the voters.

In 1969, he ran again for the city council. "I really wanted to complete the Greenbelt," he said. But his opposition called him power hungry, and Onweiler lost his council seat.[293] He did, however, serve in the Legislature until 1976[294] and while there wrote a regular column in *The Idaho Statesman* for eight years.

Interstate 80, now I-84, came to Boise in the 1960s. One of the first plans floated was to run the freeway through town and through Julia Davis Park. A storm of protest moved it to the "airport route," on the second bench, an elevated area above the river valley and about three miles south of downtown Boise.[295]

But there was still the matter of getting people from the freeway into downtown. From the time the freeway was constructed in 1961, there were discussions of a connector, an extension that would link the interstate to the business district. Once again, the parks were targeted as potential rights-of-way. One of the routes under active consideration was a corridor from the freeway along the north side of the river, across from Ann Morrison Park. "The county highway people were ready to more or less say to hell with the (fledgling) Greenbelt," said Nelson Miller.[296] The Greenbelt Committee and parks board did not view this as the best of all possible ideas.

---

293 Onweiler interview.

294 *Idaho Bluebook*, 1995-1996, comp. Secretary of State Pete Cenarrusa (State of Idaho, 1995), p. 184

295 David Proctor, "Shared Legacy," *The Idaho Statesman.*

296 Miller interview.

"Our taxes could be put to better use," argued Alice Dieter.[297]

"There were three or four alternative locations for it," said Susan Stacy, wearing her historian's hat, "and part of the chamber of commerce thought it would be a swell idea to bring it down and have it parallel the river."[298]

Once again, the Greenbelt Committee took matters into its own hands. Committee member Nelson Miller and another Greenbelt sympathizer ran for and got elected to seats on the Ada County Highway District Board of Commissioners, then killed the riverside connector. The roadway was eventually built, but it emptied traffic onto Main Street, west of downtown. Had their election bid failed, Miller said the Greenbelt Committee considered trying to broker a deal that would donate the Greenbelt property to The Nature Conservancy so the highway district would have to fight a national organization to put a highway along the Greenbelt and the river.[299]

Twenty years later, the riverside freeway idea rose yet again. The question this time was how to carry traffic efficiently, west to east across Boise, from I-184 (the Connector) near Chinden Boulevard to Broadway Avenue.

"There were a number of people who thought the right way to do it was make a nice highway right along the river," said Ken Pursley, who chaired the Greenbelt Committee during that second fight. "Fortunately, we were able to stop it."[300] The Connector now funnels traffic onto W. Myrtle Street and collects it from Front Street. These one-way thoroughfares do the job of connecting downtown and east Boise to the freeway, but they run a safe distance from the Greenbelt.

---

297 Greenbelt Committee minutes, July 1970.
298 Stacy interview.
299 Miller interview.
300 Pursley interview.

T he administration at Boise State University proved a much more difficult challenge to the Greenbelt Committee, and for many Boiseans the outcome was a good deal less satisfactory than the Connector fight.

In 1932, what would become Boise State was founded in the capital city as a private community college. In 1939, the city donated its old airport land on the south bank of the Boise River to the school, but with great foresight it retained a 100-foot easement through the property along the river. That strip subsequently became the point of strenuous debate when the school grew from junior college status to Boise State College in 1965 and to a university in 1974.

As former BSU president Dr. Charles Ruch once explained, the university saw itself as a state reservation within the city, and as such not subject to city ordinances.[301]

Like many colleges and universities situated within cities, BSU's location has made growth difficult. The river forms its north border, residential and business development grew up to the south, heavily traveled Capitol Boulevard is to the west and equally busy Broadway Avenue to the east. The cramped campus also made things difficult for the Greenbelt Committee, which wanted to impose city ordinances and use that 100-foot strip for the Greenbelt. Things were further complicated by the fact that the Greenbelt and Boise State were experiencing simultaneous growing pains. BSU is now the largest university in Idaho. While BSU's growth had an enormous positive impact on Boise, the conflicts with the Greenbelt left a bitter taste in many committee members' mouths.

One of the first BSU-Greenbelt disagreements came in 1973. As part of one of its regular meetings, the Greenbelt Committee voted to reject a recycling center on the Greenbelt, asked the Ada County

---

301   Dan Popkey, "Want to Go Nude in Boise? It's Legal on Campus," *The Idaho Statesman*, June 12, 2001, p. Local 1, June 12, 2001.

Highway District and other entities to eliminate billboards on the Greenbelt, and opposed an effort by Boise State College to locate new buildings as close as possible to the river.[302]

BSC President John Barnes Boise State University, Special Collections)

Even when BSC President John Barnes came in person to present the college's case, the committee stood its ground. It wanted to maintain the 100-foot Greenbelt easement the city had reserved through the college's property.[303] In fact, at its April 17, 1974, meeting, the committee came up with a statement of concept that said the Greenbelt, ideally, would be 600 feet wide and "conversely the inner core of the campus would visually flow to the river."[304] That rather idealistic goal was altered a month later to read that the campus should visually "flow to the Greenbelt" and the 600-foot easement was pulled back to a "100-foot Greenbelt and setback."[305]

Barnes, who made the growth of BSU a high priority, had a different plan entirely. The idea he put forth would have killed the Greenbelt, said Bill Onweiler. "He (Barnes) made plans to put the

302 Greenbelt Committee minutes, June 20, 1973 and December 19, 1973.
303 Ibid, January 1974.
304 Ibid, April 1974.
305 Ibid, May 1974.

expansion of Boise State into the Boise River," Onweiler said. "He had about ten of us out from the legislature to show us this wonderful plan at lunch, which showed a row of buildings out about 20, 30 feet into the river on stilts. That way he could expand without having to buy ground on the other side."

Onweiler, who was no longer a city official, alerted the Greenbelt Committee. "Somehow that plan disappeared and never was mentioned again," he said. "I couldn't believe he thought he could do that."[306]

"The question was," said committee member Jeanne Lundell, who has also served on the BSU alumni board, "did Boise City have control of the setback or did the state of Idaho have control of the setback? Once they built the corner of a building out into the setback. The university had a tendency to go ahead and do things and then ask permission."

For instance, Lundell said, BSU installed light poles without permission near Christ Chapel and the Broadway underpass on the east end of the campus, not far from what is now Albertsons Stadium. Then the university found out the Boise Parks & Recreation Department staff was in the process of redesigning that area, and the lights had to be taken out.

"There was always something – nit, nit, nit, nit, nit – between the two," Lundell said. "But I didn't feel that BSU should be treated any differently than any other person coming before the committee asking permission."[307]

"My biggest disappointment was Boise State University," said Elizabeth Van Zonneveld. "My husband was a professor there. I really thought better of the university, of the personnel, including Dr. John Barnes. But he turned out to be very selfish about the river. The

---

306 Onweiler interview.
307 Jeanne Lundell interview with Troy Reeves, Boise, Idaho; July 9, 1998.

university has not been as accommodating, and the things that happened there set an example.

"I understand they have a very tight place and not a lot of room to grow. But trying to grow into the (Julia Davis) park across the river and continually pressing, disregarding the public, I was pretty disappointed that the university was very selfish when it came to considering the needs of the city as a whole along the river and the stretch it occupied."[308]

Her feelings were echoed by Greenbelt Committee members Bob Whipkey, Bert Cleaveland and Mike Misner. Though Jack Cooper got along well with BSU President John Keiser, who succeeded Barnes, Van Zonneveld, Whipkey, Cleaveland and Misner all point to BSU as a large pebble in the committee's hiking boot.

BSU President John Keiser, 1981 (Boise State University, Special Collections)

"They were fairly unresponsive to our requests that they keep us in the loop," said Whipkey, who served on the committee from 1994 to 1997. "They would tell us one thing, go ahead, and do whatever they felt like doing. They didn't think they had to deal with us or pay any

---

308 Van Zonneveld interview.

attention to us or follow any of our recommendations. It became very, very frustrating for us."[309]

"I think the university made a terrible error all through the time when I was on the committee when they did not apply the same rules to their part of it as we did to the rest," said Robert Stolz in 1998. "It is by far the worst section of the Greenbelt. If you walk there today it's kind of a rotten-looking thing, and it could have been, or should have been, a major feature, a selling point, a reason to go to Boise State. We were jacked around by the university at every turn. Although from time to time they talked a good talk, I have yet to see them walk the walk. And in general, Boise State somehow doesn't think they're part of the community of Boise. I feel fairly strongly about that, but so has everyone who has ever been acquainted with this."[310]

An additional point of conflict was Barnes' proposal in the late 1970s to build a walking bridge, later named the Bob Gibb Friendship Bridge, across the river to Julia Davis Park.

Greenbelt member David Collins remembers Barnes presenting the idea to the committee. One of the questions asked of Barnes was, "Wouldn't that bridge turn Julia Davis Park into a BSU parking lot?' And he said, 'Definitely not,' said Collins.[311]

Nancy Donald also opposed the bridge. "I was very anti that because we were afraid it would just turn Julia Davis Park into a parking lot for Boise State College, and that's definitely what happened."[312]

Still, the committee as a whole sided with BSU and recommended the city approve the bridge.

---

309   Bob Whipkey interview with Troy Reeves, Boise, Idaho; August 11, 1998.

310   Robert Stolz interview with Troy Reeves, Boise, Idaho; June 9, 1998.

311   David Collins interview with Troy Reeves, Boise, Idaho; July 30, 1998.

312   Donald interview.

Donald was outspoken on several Greenbelt Committee issues. She opposed the bridge and many other BSU infringements on the river – including the Morrison Center. Later she also spoke out against the committee's loss of power over the last 10 years of its existence. Her forthright approach, Donald said, was not looked upon kindly at City Hall. "The only time I felt that we were ignored or shelved was the situation with Boise State College," she said. In the 1990s, after years of making her opinions known on those issues, she said that she was told, via the mayor and (Parks director) Jim Hall, "to keep my mouth shut about the college infringing on the river."

Donald is the only committee member to say she was gagged, but the Greenbelt-BSU conflict may have cost one Greenbelt Committee member some important work. Nelson Miller was an architect who served on the committee in the early 1970s and believed strongly in the Greenbelt concept. He said his work on the committee was not "for myself or for my children or for my grandchildren. I was working on this Greenbelt because once it's established it will be there forever, for hundreds of years, and any violation and any special consideration we gave to one person or group of people to let it within 25 feet would not only set the precedent for other people to come within 25 feet, but that violation would be there forever. I felt we had an obligation to ourselves and the subsequent generations for time and eternity to do it right and take our lumps. And indeed I did take my lumps."[313]

During his time on the committee, Miller, who had already designed several campus buildings, vied with two other firms for a chance to design the Morrison Center for the Performing Arts, which was to be located on the BSU campus. He had earlier supported the committee's decision to deny both firms a variance to encroach on the Greenbelt, and Miller believes his role on the committee eliminated his chance to work on the new building.

---

313 Miller interview.

The Greenbelt volunteers not only spent considerable amounts of their own time at meetings to make acquisitions and review plans; not only did they lead clean-up efforts and lobby behind the scenes; but some were willing to risk their own financial futures.

The Barber Lumber Company built Barber Dam east of Boise, downstream from Diversion Dam. Construction began in 1903 and the 25-foot-high, rock-filled dam was complete in 1905. The lumber mill was built in 1906. The town of Barberton, later shortened to Barber, was built at the same time and grew to 650 residents. It was the last mill town in Idaho. Barber was a self-sufficient company town – 18 square blocks, a sewer and water system, a school district, company-owned hotel and community hall, and a dam with a power plant. For a time, it was the second largest town in Ada County.[314]

After a short but productive life, the Barber mill closed in 1935, the railway that served it was abandoned, and what was left of the town and mill were razed and salvaged in 1935-36. The dam, however, remained, and began to deteriorate.[315]

Nelson Miller and John Chapman, who served as the Planning and Zoning Commission's representative on the Greenbelt Committee for eight years in the 1970s, remember the story well.

Barber Dam was owned by an individual who hadn't paid his taxes, and the dam was on the block at a sheriff's sale. No local government wanted to take on the aging structure, and the Greenbelt Committee worried that unless a public body acquired ownership and repaired it, the dam would wash out and destroy all the wonderful wildlife habitat downstream. The muddy sediment from such a washout, said Miller, would also force the canal companies that depended on the dam to either shut off canals or let them fill with

---

314 Witherell, *History Along the Greenbelt*, pp. 22-23.
315 Ibid, p. 26.

mud. Either action would cut off irrigation water to most of Ada and Canyon counties.

A group of the Greenbelt members, working independently of the committee, decided it had to act. In much the same way Nelson Miller got elected to the Ada County Highway District board and diverted the freeway, Chapman, an attorney, formed the Boise River Conservancy. Funded by Art Troutner, Gay Davis and a few others, this nonprofit corporation went to the tax sale and bought the dam for between $3,500 and $5,000. Their hope was that the city, county or state would recognize the need and take it off their hands in order to preserve the wildlife and ensure the reliability of the irrigation system.

It was a gamble, and they were playing with real money. After the expense of the purchase, the group members couldn't afford to repair the dam, and if it failed they feared their liability could total $5 million. For a time, it looked like a losing bet. Government at every level declined to take responsibility for the dam. Fortunately, the group made up in creativity what it lacked in cash. The ingenious solution: It simply refused to pay taxes for a few years and forced the county to foreclose. Once it owned it, the county had to repair it. "Now it's a tremendous part of the Boise River Greenbelt system," said Chapman.[316]

Morrison-Knudsen Corporation and co-founder Harry Morrison were directly involved with the Boise River since the company's early days building irrigation canals. MK and Morrison began to affect the future creation of the Greenbelt in the 1940s when Morrison's Southwest Idaho Water Conservation Project lobbied for Lucky Peak Dam. It was the dams, after all, that controlled the river, which allowed people to use the floodplain in new and imaginative ways. Later, the company donated

316 Chapman interview.

the east end of Julia Davis Park,[317] from east of the tennis courts to what became Broadway Avenue;[318] the Harry Morrison Family Foundation created Ann Morrison Park; and the company funded the Morrison-Knudsen Nature Center adjacent to Municipal Park.

In 1976, the company again became an active player in the Greenbelt game when Emkay, Morrison-Knudsen's development arm, proposed to develop about 125 acres east of Broadway Avenue and on the south bank of the Boise River. The company asked Boise to annex the property, which was only about a mile from downtown. ParkCenter, as that part of Boise is now called, was at the time "several depleted gravel pits and other land," said Susan Stacy,[319] but MK had plans to convert the property into a high-quality office park.

The negotiations got off to a good start. Boise City owned a three-acre peninsula of land that jutted into the Emkay property, and the company proposed to trade that land for about the same acreage along the river for a Greenbelt easement and to donate a park. The city agreed. In 1977, when combined with property the city already owned, Boise suddenly had almost a mile of new Greenbelt access and a renovated gravel pit that is now ParkCenter Park and ParkCenter Pond.[320]

After that, things got a bit more complicated. Though the ordinance was not yet approved, the Boise City Council had recently adopted a policy that expressed its "intent" to prohibit construction in the floodway. Nearly all the ParkCenter property was in the floodplain and the majority was in the floodway. An additional complication was that Boise was a participant in the federal government's National Flood Insurance Program, which did not allow construction in the floodway.

---

317 Witherell, *History Along the Greenbelt*, p. 84

318 Cooper, written comments, p. 4

319 Stacy, *When the River Rises*, p. 83

320 Ibid, pp. 84-85.

For a number of reasons, the city council decided to approve the project. As the council members saw it, a land swap between Boise and Emkay would give the city nearly a mile of Greenbelt property if the development were approved.

They also reasoned that downtown was tied up in the seemingly endless urban renewal-downtown mall question, so there was no land there for new corporate offices. Albertsons supermarket chain and other companies wanted to build headquarters buildings, and ParkCenter offered the chance for Boise to control the development of those offices and to prevent them from going outside the city. The concentration of businesses on ParkCenter Boulevard also kept open the option of mass transit along that corridor.

And finally, despite the floodway problems, ParkCenter Boulevard was the key access road to opening the entire East Boise area to development.

The council's approval came even though it had no idea how to solve the floodplain problems, and the fact that it had to seek the Army Corps of Engineers' comments before it made a final decision.

The Corps, however, refused to approve Emkay's proposal, and a long conversation began between engineers from Boise, Emkay and the Corps. There were also lengthy negotiations between Boise's and Emkay's attorneys over the Greenbelt setback. "Emkay fought us tooth and nail," said John Chapman. "They were thinking they were going to have a restaurant that was going to be built on pylons over the Boise River or overlooking the river. They were very much opposed to our 50-foot setback ordinance. They hired lawyers to fight us, and they put up a real battle. Of course, they also organized some of the other property owners along there to fight us."

Boise won that setback battle, as it had won the earlier ones, and Chapman said a few years later: "I think Morrison-Knudsen today would be one of the first corporations to admit the Greenbelt is a wonderful concept and has really improved the value of their property."[321]

Emkay fared better in the city and the Army Corps offices. The company agreed to build a levee on the south side of the river, and to ensure there would be no resultant flooding on the north side, to build a channel – actually a slight depression – through ParkCenter that in the case of a flood would divert enough water to keep the river from overflowing the opposite bank.[322]

Emkay and Boise got ParkCenter, Boise controlled the development and everyone got the Greenbelt. ParkCenter also demonstrated that large commercial developers were convinced the river and the Greenbelt were now attractive places to build.[323]

So attractive, in fact, that the Broadway Avenue underpass on the south bank of the river was built in 1983-84 to accommodate the foot and bike traffic between the ParkCenter area and Boise State University.[324] The underpass is being rebuilt in 2016 as part of the Broadway Bridge reconstruction.

Until ParkCenter, large developers had stayed away from the Greenbelt, said Susan Stacy. Only after Emkay showed it would work, and the Greenbelt proved to be a hit, did big builders begin to get into the game. "Then, the property next to the river became more interesting and more valuable. I really don't see them as ever having promoted it, or gotten in the way of it, or given it a thought. I didn't see their names at public hearings, I didn't see them playing any role at all because nobody had the idea of developing anything interesting or important along the river until the Greenbelt was *a fait accompli* and continuing to grow," she said.

---

321 Chapman interview.

322 Stacy, *When the River Rises*, pp. 85-86.

323 Dieter interview.

324 Jack Cooper, "Boise Greenbelt Capital Projects of the 80s," unpublished written comments, p. 1.

"Once the developers began developing, there was a good deal more struggle about this interface between the public and private, and who's going to own the river, who's going to have practical access to the river. After ParkCenter came Plantation, Glenwood Village and River Run. But the first time I remember a sense of conflict over access to the river was probably with River Run."[325]

---

325 Stacy interview.

7 The Great River Run Debate

"I regret that the original (Greenbelt) ideal was broken at River Run."

– Susan Stacy

"If you look at the public opinion polls about where the nicest stretch of the Greenbelt is, it's that (River Run) stretch we're talking about."

– Peter O'Neill, River Run developer

River

Run, more than two decades after it was finished and sold out, is still the most complicated, debated and misunderstood development along Boise's Greenbelt. Arguments over the divided Greenbelt path that began there still engender hard feelings on both sides.

The property is 118 acres located in East Boise beyond ParkCenter on the south side of the Boise River, across from the Warm Springs Golf Club.

"We bought it from a group of 13 doctors and an undertaker in 1978," said Peter O'Neill, founder of O'Neill Enterprises, Inc. The medical group had gotten itself in a financial bind and wanted to sell. The property was "overgrazed pasture and a lot of dead cottonwoods," he said. Cattle had broken down the riparian edges, and there was riprap in the river, but the land was salvageable and the most polluted stretches of the river were farther west.[326]

Peter O'Neill, 1982. (Idaho Statesman)

O'Neill's proposal was to build 635 units – a mix of apartments, condominiums and single-family homes – as a planned-unit development. It was to be the first planned residential community in Boise. To accomplish that, he had to overcome two large obstacles – the lack of access to the property and the fact that the floodplain covered much of the River Run property.

To solve the access problem, O'Neill's company extended ParkCenter Boulevard, or the Southeast Collector as it was called early on, about sixth-tenths of a mile from Mallard Drive to River Run and conveyed it to the Ada County Highway District.[327] The

326 Peter O'Neill, interview with the author, Boise, Idaho; January 19, 2001.
327 O'Neill interview.

floodplain discussion, as it did with the ParkCenter development, just downstream from River Run, involved the developer, the city and the Army Corps of Engineers. Again, the city wanted to promote development in East Boise and again it passed the flood-control problem on to the Corps. River Run engineers did a very detailed study of the property and prepared documentation to demonstrate that the floodplain was less extensive than shown by the broader study the Corps had done earlier. The Army Corps accepted the new floodplain map but, as it had with Emkay at ParkCenter, asked River Run to create another floodway on its property to ensure the floodwaters would not be pushed to the other side of the river. River Run agreed to carve a new channel out of its property. The problem was, that channel would come out of land that had been proposed for a swap with the city.

Again, as with Emkay, Boise was willing to trade about four acres of its excess parkland to River Run in exchange for Greenbelt acreage. River Run would get a portion of what was then Loggers Park and is now Baggley Park to use for access into its development, and Boise would get about eight acres of Greenbelt property. Unfortunately, Boise was about to discover that the devil is indeed in the details. The fine print the city overlooked was that, because it had purchased the parkland with the Department of Interior's Land and Water Conservation funds, it had to obtain approval from both the Interior Department and the state's Heritage Conservation and Recreation Fund, which administered the money, before any change was made in ownership. No one on the Greenbelt Committee, which approved the swap, caught this omission. Neither did Doug Erdman, the Greenbelt Coordinator at the time, or the city parks or planning staffs.[328]

It took until 1987 for all the legal knots to be untangled, and for Boise to get the approvals it needed.[329]

---

328 Stacy, *When the River Rises*, pp. 88-91.
329 Greenbelt Committee minutes, Sept. 10, 1987.

In the meantime, O'Neill was under financial pressure and needed
to proceed. And the Greenbelt sat stalled at the entrance to River Run
while the parks department spent its severely stretched budget on
other parts of the path.[330]

During the River Run negotiations, O'Neill insisted he owed the
city less Greenbelt land. He argued that some of the city's property
would be eaten up by the flood-control channels and the new Lake
Heron, another flood control feature River Run had created. The
riverfront land he was giving up, he argued, was more valuable than
the landlocked parcel Boise had. The city agreed and took less
Greenbelt property.

Still, Wayne Gibbs, at the time Boise's director of Community
Planning and Development, described the land swap as "just a real
steal for the city."[331]

And O'Neill said, "Frankly, I thought we got screwed on that
thing, but there wasn't a whole lot you could do about it."[332]

Despite the ongoing disagreements and land-swap problems, there
were several reasons Boise was willing to come to an agreement with
O'Neill. For one, the city wanted to control the development and
extend sewer lines into Southeast Boise. For another, Boise City,
along with every other taxing entity in the state, had been staggered
by the One Percent Tax Limitation Initiative passed in 1978. Modeled
on California's famous Proposition 13, the One Percent proposed to
limit property taxes to one percent of market value. Although the
initiative passed, it posed a hornet's nest of legal problems and was
never fully implemented. The Legislature did, however, adopt parts of
the measure, and the modified One Percent still imposed serious
financial restrictions on how quickly city budgets could rise.

---

330 Stacy, *When the River Rises*, p. 91.
331 Gibbs interview.
332 O'Neill interview.

As longtime Idaho political journalist Randy Stapilus wrote in his book *Paradox Politics: People and Power in Idaho*: "In the late seventies local governments made tremendous cuts in services, some wiping out whole departments. Maintenance of buildings and other services fell by the wayside."[333]

In 1980, already desperate for income, Ada County, along with the rest of the state and much of the country, suffered another economic blow – a serious recession. "We hit the worst building cycle and economic cycle this town had ever seen in the early '80s," said O'Neill. "Ada County and all the cities in it went from 2,900 housing starts in 1979 to 400 in 1981. That's when interest rates went to 20%. That was a tough period of time, but character building."[334]

"Up to 1980, Boise was hopping," former planner Susan Stacy said. "In 1981 or '82, things collapsed. The planning department worked on churches and daycare centers, not subdivisions."[335]

"More people were moving out than moving in," said Wayne Gibbs. "We had one of the few markets in the country with declining real estate values. The city, when they had a chance to get some upscale development of any kind, was a little more cooperative and willing to bend the rules than it is now."[336]

And at the same time, Boise City government was still preoccupied with the Sisyphean problem of downtown redevelopment and its futile efforts to find a developer to build a downtown mall. "The (downtown) mall was the number one issue, the number two issue and the number three issue," said Stacy. "The city government and staff were devoted to the mall. If not for that, maybe more attention would have been paid to River Run."[337]

---

333 Stapilus, *Paradox Politics,* p. 259.
334 O'Neill interview.
335 Stacy interview.
336 Gibbs interview.
337 Stacy interview.

Whether the turmoil caused by the One Percent, the recession and downtown redevelopment played a role in the Greenbelt negotiations with River Run is impossible to say. Stacy believes they were contributing factors to the lack of communication she feels resulted in the hotly debated split Greenbelt path at River Run. O'Neill contends the split path was exactly what city officials wanted.

Whichever the case, it was during this period O'Neill and the Greenbelt Committee were in negotiations over the path. Not whether it would go through River Run – the Greenbelt was too well established to debate at that point – but what it would look like.

I n her book, *When the River Rises*, Stacy writes that the original agreement between River Run and the Greenbelt Committee was that there would be a Greenbelt walking path along the river the length of the development, that the setback would be variable distances from the river, and that River Run would provide a bike path but would locate it "partially in the Greenbelt and partially through the project, away from the river." But by the time the land swap was untangled and the flood-control channels were built, the original agreement had changed. River Run proposed and later built a "delineated bike path" – a striped bike lane – on River Run Drive.[338]

O'Neill says the idea of a pedestrian-only path came from the city, not him. "One of the first things I did was meet with the Greenbelt Committee, and there was a strong sentiment on the part of the committee that they would like to see a stretch of the Greenbelt left in its natural condition, without a paved bike path," he said.[339]

"I think the mission statement has always been to save public access for people along the river," said longtime committee member

---

338 Stacy, *When the River Rises*, p. 89.
339 O'Neill interview.

Nancy Donald. "That doesn't mean it has to be a paved trail or mowed grass."[340]

Doubtless, it didn't hurt that O'Neill's attorney for these negotiations was former Greenbelt Committee chair Ken Pursley.[341]

Of course, the "natural condition" of that stretch of river wasn't any more attractive than it had been downstream when the Greenbelt started, O'Neill conceded. What he, Greenbelt Coordinator Doug Erdman and the committee decided to pursue was "an improved natural state," he said, one with wetlands and plant growth that would attract wildlife. As for the idea that the city would simply impose its setback and extend the bike path through River Run, "We just never went there," he said.

"In simple terms, the notion was to keep it in its natural state, have a gravel path that would be a walking pedestrian path, and take the bike path off the river and find some other route," said O'Neill, "so ultimately the bike path would parallel the river and meet a target somewhere down at Barber Park, which would ultimately get linked up to the rest of the system. So we did that. We thought that was a good planning concept. We made River Run Drive extra wide for the delineated bike paths on either side of it.

"We worked together on it, but the goal was, can you get the bike path off the river and leave just the pedestrian path along the river?" O'Neill continued. "Which I didn't fight, by the way. I thought that was a good thing to do. At the time, I don't recall a lot of debate as to whether that was a good or bad idea. There wasn't a lot of debate, either, over the delineated bike paths, even though that was a new idea. The whole concept worked, and all the appropriate agencies blessed it."[342]

---

340 Donald interview.

341 Pursley interview.

342 O'Neill interview.

O'Neill points out that early in the Greenbelt's creation there was a debate about whether it would be a passive park or a pathway. The pathway proponents won the argument, but there were still people who wanted a more "natural" look and feel, at least in parts.

"The thinking was, 'Wait a minute. What we're really going to end up with is a Greenbelt-bike path, a linear manicured park along the river,' the developer said. "Is that really what we want, from a community standpoint? Should we have a section that is a little harder to get to, that if you wanted to take the extra energy and take your kid for a walk, or go fishing, or do something that will be a little bit more like walking along a river, as opposed to walking in a park in the city? That had a very good ring to people, and it was still only a couple miles from downtown Boise, so you could still take your bike and go wherever you wanted to go."

Nancy Donald said most of the Greenbelt Committee felt that way. "I think the proposal was made to us in the fall of '78, and that winter we worked on it," she said. "I felt it was an asset to the community, and that Pete O'Neill was doing a good job of engineering it and laying it out. I looked at more than just where the Greenbelt was going. We decided not to have a path run right next to the river, that we'd keep the bicycles off of it and it would be just a pedestrian path. The Greenbelt didn't mean a path or a trail, it meant public access to the river, and it still does to me."[343]

Nelson Miller, on the other hand, describes River Run as the worst decision he saw in 10 years on the committee. Most of the members were against the idea initially, Miller said, and he was away teaching at the University of Idaho in Moscow. But Greenbelt Coordinator Doug Erdman "gave an impassioned speech" in favor of O'Neill's plan and it was accepted, even though it was "against the principles we had established originally," said Miller.[344]

---

343 Donald interview.
344   Miller interview.

Alice Dieter echoed Miller when she said: "I think the city lost tremendously when Mayor Dick Eardley let Pete O'Neill take the bike path off the river."[345]

Mayor Richard R. Eardley, 1974-86. (Boise City Department of Arts & History)

Stacy, Boise's city planner at the time, sees the split path at River Run as the result of a communication breakdown within the city government. Mayor Dick Eardley and new parks director Jack Cooper, who inherited many of the River Run issues, were having separate conversations with O'Neill and the many city departments involved in the development. But none of those departments were talking to each other, she said.

"The mayor never got all of the department heads who were involved in this together," said Stacy. "It would have been nice if the mayor had called all of us together one day and said, 'Look here. What's happening? What are we doing?' But he didn't do that, so some of these negotiations took place without the other city employees being aware of them. There really was no opportunity for a unified set of city departments to be moving along on the same foot. The city engineer, the public works department, was interested in the

345   Dieter interview

flood control issue. It wasn't their charter to be worried about the Greenbelt.

"I don't think anybody bent any rules," said Stacy, who doesn't blame the mayor. "Eardley just didn't think this wasn't going to turn out alright." She added: "The park board failed big time" and that she personally feels "a great sense of loss."[346]

The end result, in Stacy's view, was the Greenbelt was sacrificed. O'Neill, not surprisingly, disagrees, and Jack Cooper added: "Susan Stacy's viewpoint is by far the minority,"[347] something Stacy readily acknowledges.[348]

Stacy, however, writes in her book that in 1986, at least some people's sentiment matched her own as the public began to become aware of what she describes as "the city's quiet negotiations" with River Run, the divided pathway and the problematic land trades. Stacy quotes Jim Floros' letter to the editor of *The Idaho Statesman*: "I am appalled that our local government has allowed a developer to move into an area on our river and develop homes at a profit, at the expense of our community needs. I don't remember at any time that we were asked if it was all right to give up the banks of our river to private use, but this is what has happened at River Run. Our brightest city accent, the bike path, has actually been eliminated from the river for several years."

Numerous letters followed, most in the same vein.[349] But as late as 1987, the Greenbelt Committee discussed the issue and remained firm that the path should be a soft surface along the river and that bikes would have a separate right-of-way on the subdivision streets.[350] Nevertheless, negotiations over the final details of access and bridge construction continued until 1989.

---

346 Stacy interview.
347 Cooper, written comments, p. 6.
348 Stacy interview.
349 Stacy, *When the River Rises*, p. 93 and p. 161.
350 Greenbelt Committee minutes, Jan. 15, 1987.

O'Neill points out correctly that the banks of the river through
River Run were private property. He also notes that River Run went
through the entire public hearing process and passed muster with the
Greenbelt Committee and the city council.

"I just totally, absolutely disagree with her, with the spin she put on
it," O'Neill said of Stacy's book. "Clearly, in those days the public
hearings were not as well attended, were not as well advertised as they
are today. But I think the city met all the criteria for posting, and you
could go and look at the plans and go to the meetings."[351]

For her part, Stacy said she took the idea seriously that the
Greenbelt should be a path that separated people from automobiles.
She wanted to see the path go the length of the river and never make
riders or walkers have to cross a street.

"I regret that the original ideal was broken at River Run," she said.
"I've also noted that not very many other people have the same regret
I do. I have the impression a lot of the planners who came after I left
(the city) thought there was nothing wrong with this, that there was
nothing wrong with having a pedestrian section along the river and a
bike section along the road. That it was better for the environment.
But I never accepted it. And I regret very much that it happened. It's
not the same. You just can't get off your bike and walk down by the
river. It's not a natural thing to do. I think the public has less than
what it deserves. River Run, and the flood control necessity, just blew
everything else away."[352]

Replies O'Neill: "If you look at the public opinion polls about
where the nicest stretch of the Greenbelt is, it's that stretch we're
talking about. There's no question in my mind that it's a tremendous
benefit to the city. I don't think we need 28 miles of wilderness along
the river through a metro area, but I'm not sure 28 miles of asphalt
with some grass on it is appropriate, either. I like the feel of the

---

351 O'Neill interview.
352 Stacy interview.

walking path, and I think what they've done on the other side of the river, with the golf course and the riparian areas, makes good sense, too."[353]

Wayne Gibbs, former director of Boise Community Planning and Development, offers the closest thing to a neutral perspective on this still-debated issue. First, he said, the city got what it wanted, which was an extensive piece of land along the river that it might not have gotten otherwise. Second, "there's nothing to prevent the city from going back and paving that section if it wants." Third, he likes the walking path and thinks there is a lot of public support for having pieces of the Greenbelt more natural and passive and preserved for pedestrians only.[354]

In 1990, River Run won an Award of Excellence from the Urban Land Institute. On the plaque that hangs in O'Neill's office, the ULI stated: "The developer's attention to detail and commitment to quality and the environment have created a premier planned development that serves as an example to the entire region.

O'Neill followed River Run with what, if anything, was a more controversial planned development. Spring Meadow is 350 units, all single-family, built in two phases on 80-plus acres located along the river east of River Run. O'Neill purchased some of the land from Keith Gilmore, a former Greenbelt Committee member.

The approval process went much more quickly than with River Run. Though there was another national recession in the early 1990s, Boise's increasingly high-tech economy was hardly affected. Spring Meadow sold out quickly.

Once again, O'Neill and the city, this time in the person of parks director Jack Cooper, engineered a land swap. But the biggest, or at least the most public, issue that faced O'Neill and the city this time was parking. Spring Meadow's streets were built to be narrow and

---

353 O'Neill interview.
354 Gibbs interview.

private, which precluded public parking. That made it hard for people from other parts of Boise to drive there, park and get to the river and the Greenbelt.

"That's one hundred percent by design," said O'Neill. "And the city was totally, one hundred percent aware. Everybody was on board with it."[355]

The decision to make the streets private was based on the Ada County Highway District's requirement that all subdivision streets be 36 feet wide. Spring Meadow, said O'Neill, was designed so the side streets served only 20 to 30 homes each and therefore did not need 36 feet of pavement. In order to build 32-foot streets, the roadways had to be private. But the narrow streets rule out parking on both sides and eliminated public parking within the subdivision altogether.

"It wasn't made for public parking," said O'Neill. "We knew Riverside School was coming, so there would be parking there. Baggley Park has parking and a pathway from there to the river. It's a quarter-mile walk to the Greenbelt from the park or the school. We also put in handicapped parking as close as we could get it to the Greenbelt, and there are paths throughout our property that allow public access to the river."

Not surprisingly, the issue turned out to be not quite that simple. In 1991, O'Neill wanted to post no-parking signs in Spring Meadow. The Planning and Zoning Commission denied the request on the grounds it would limit access to the Greenbelt, and in August, the city council denied O'Neill's appeal.[356] He also ran into a public that was now well aware of the split path in River Run and the new proposal to keep the Greenbelt and bike path separate through Spring Meadow. Walkers liked the idea. Cyclists didn't. Both sides were quite vocal. All the while O'Neill tried to remind the city that this stretch of river was supposed to be a little less accessible than Ann Morrison Park.

---

355 O'Neill interview.
356 Greenbelt Committee minutes, July 11, 1991.

"It was not designed for the general public to pull up and pull out a picnic and walk down to the river," he said. "Those hearings were just unbelievable. Nobody wanted to talk about the merits of the project."[357]

Greenbelt member David Jones, who joined the committee in 1996, remained concerned about parking availability near the Greenbelt from Broadway Avenue east. "In southeast Boise, if you didn't have the parking lots of the headquarters buildings (on ParkCenter Boulevard) for Albertsons and (the former) Ore-Ida (building, now occupied by Boise State Radio), your parking spaces are very limited. Suppose those people said, 'We're not going to let you park in there anymore?' Spring Meadow I and II have very limited access and very limited parking. Baggley Park provides some parking, as does Riverside School, but the walking pathway is quite a distance from the bicycling pathway and subsequently I don't think it is used as much by the majority of people from Boise because it is a little bit of a hassle to get to."[358]

Stacy contrasts Spring Meadow to what was done with other projects, such as the Bach's building on 13th Street near Shoreline Park. The Greenbelt Committee asked the Bach's developer hard questions about how people would get around that building to the river. "That was apparently one of the conditions of approval, that the public would have access to the river from some point in the parking lot – forever. Period. There was no pussyfooting around that."[359]

The access debate continued. Greenbelt users voiced frustration that the East Park Center Bridge east of Spring Meadow eliminated the few parking places between Riverside School and the river that have been used for nearly a decade.[360]

---

357 O'Neill interview.

358 Jones interview.

359 Stacy interview.

360 Emily Simnitt, "New Bridge Will Cut Parking Options Along Greenbelt," *The Idaho Statesman*, p. 1B, December 16, 2000.

T
he land swap at Spring Meadow went better than the River
Run snafu but was far from smooth. The city had 11.2 acres
then known as Loggers Park that it wanted to develop into
Baggley Park near Spring Meadow, but it only needed eight. At the
time, the average Boise neighborhood park was 7.5 acres. O'Neill had
riverfront land the city wanted for the Greenbelt. As with the previous
case, the city had used federal Land and Water Conservation Funds to
purchase the parkland and needed federal and state agency approvals
to make the exchange.

The appraisals were made and this time the city got the necessary
approvals. Boise, after a great deal of discussion and several public
hearings, traded five acres of its excess park property for about 16
acres of riverfront land for the Greenbelt.[361]

"The exchange was a pretty long, drawn-out process because part
of the public didn't think the city should trade away a part of the
public park in order to get Greenbelt along the river," said Wayne
Gibbs, "even though the city was very careful to get appraisals and
document that the value of the land we were getting was worth much
more than the land we were giving away. Plus, they didn't trade all of
Baggley Park. They traded part of it, so the city wound up with a
neighborhood park plus a number of miles of additional Greenbelt
area that they did not have before. The developer took the piece he got
and developed it into residential lots, but in exchange the city got
probably one of the biggest chunks of Greenbelt frontage we've ever
gotten.

"It was just a real steal for the city, but in those days the public was
suspicious of any dealings directly between the city and developers,
so a lot of people thought it was a clandestine plot or something. But
it did work out in the long run," said Gibbs. "The city felt because of
all the plans that had been put in place and the work of the Greenbelt

---

361 Cooper, written comments, p.5.

committee and the parks department, it was imperative that we acquire those stretches of the Greenbelt."[362]

After the River Run fiasco, however, O'Neill did not trust the parks department or Director Jack Cooper. In 1986, he took the Spring Meadow land exchange documents directly to Mayor Dirk Kempthorne and asked him to co-sign. "I said, 'If we have any deal, you're going to sign it. I want somebody else's neck in the noose'," said O'Neill.[363]

"O'Neill caught a lot of flack, some of it probably justified and a lot of it not," said Gibbs, "but he does quality developments. And he will go by the rules, but you have to show him that there are rules and it's not just something you want. He wants to see it in writing."[364]

Stacy, who describes herself as populist, argued: "I don't like it that the very wealthy people have access to the river and that they organize and attempt to keep the rest of the public out."[365]

O'Neill dismisses many of these arguments as "revisionist history." "Frankly," said O'Neill, "I get as upset as hell when all the do-gooders come out of the woodwork and say, 'Hey, you screwed over the city. It's a rich developer developing ground for rich property owners, and the public has been blocked off the river.' Well, I say there's absolutely no question, there's public access in Spring Meadow. Yes, these are private roads, but here's the public access as well.

"Maybe the divided path was a bad decision. Maybe it was bad public policy. But it was public policy, and it was done in the full light of day in the midst of this enormous argument. It ranged from some who said there shouldn't be any development on the Greenbelt, no path whatsoever, to it should be paved, to it should be 12 feet of

---

362 Gibbs interview.
363 O'Neill interview.
364 Gibbs interview.
365 Stacy interview.

pavement, to it should be parallel paths. I remember the Happy Hoofers (walking group). They were our allies. They said it should be a walking path. 'The bikers have their path,' they said, 'this is our path.' It's unfortunate that it became a lightning-rod issue, but because it was a lightning-rod issue this whole business of public access was thoroughly aired."

O'Neill also argues that a pedestrian-only path was the right way to go. "If you stop and think about it, a walking-only path is still good public policy," he said. "If the 20-something miles of Greenbelt was continuous access and it was all within 100 yards of public parking, it wouldn't be the experience it is today. The whole notion of it is that there should be a couple miles of it that is a little harder to access. It's going to be a little different experience than walking through Julia Davis Park or Ann Morrison Park. I think that's a good thing."

It is true, he conceded, that a person on a bike can't ride from one end of the Greenbelt to the other and stay near the river. But he insisted: "Look, as a biker you've got 25 out of 28 miles that you're on the river. Why not give pedestrians the courtesy of having X percent that was more or less designed for them?"[366]

River Run is not alone in that respect. The path through the Warm Springs Golf Club is also off the river, said Jack Cooper.[367]

While Stacy worried about the precedent River Run and Spring Meadow might have set for then-future developments such as Harris Ranch, on the east end of the Greenbelt,[368] O'Neill dismisses that concern. "I don't believe we've set a precedent," he said. "If the city council deems in its wisdom that what was done at River Run and Spring Meadow was a mistake, well just because they allowed it to happen then doesn't mean we have to make the same mistake again."[369]

366 O'Neill interview.
367 Cooper, written comments, p. 7.
368 Stacy interview.
369 O'Neill interview.

In fact, the current comprehensive plan did not continue the restriction on paved paths within the setback.[370]

O ne of the most significant problems facing the Greenbelt Committee and the city during the trail's expansion in the 1980s was how to get it under existing thoroughfares so users did not have to cross busy streets. The Main Street tunnel was built in September 1982 to enable Greenbelt users to connect safely with Veterans State Park. Jack Cooper described it as "perhaps the most significant capital improvement and one of the major trail safety enhancement projects."[371]

To pull it off with the least amount of inconvenience to commuter traffic, the city parks department and state transportation department agreed to a precise weekend schedule. The September date was chosen to take advantage of low water flows in the river. Large-diameter pipe was shipped to the site in advance. Main Street was closed on a Friday night after the commute, and crews worked for 60 hours straight to install, bolt together and waterproof the pipe. Traffic was able to drive over the tunnel only 15 minutes later than planned.

The Greenbelt, of course, was moving west as well. The chief problem in that direction was the opposite of the eastward expansion: Many of the developments were already in place and had to be retrofitted to accommodate the pathway. Two of the most difficult potholes for the committee to navigate were the residential area known as Willow Lane and the planned residential and business development Lake Harbor. Willow Lane, also known as Heron Hollow, proved to be such a roadblock that the committee skipped it for a time in order to focus its attention on Lake Harbor, even though Lake Harbor was farther west.

---

370 Gibbs interview.
371 Cooper, "Capital Projects," p.1.

That is not to say Lake Harbor was a picnic. "There was a lot of resistance to the Greenbelt in the late 1980s," said member Joe LaMarche. "Lake Harbor put a lot of pressure on the parks department and the Greenbelt Committee to narrow the amount of property available for the pathway between the edge of the (Lake Harbor) pond and the river. It was a bit of a battle."[372]

The planning difficulties were multiplied by Lake Harbor's ownership changes. Jim Kalbus, who was on the committee at the time, says Lake Harbor was the most important achievement in his nine years of service. The sticking point was the acquisition of property, Kalbus said. The original owner went bankrupt, and the new owner wasn't aware of commitments made by the earlier owner.[373]

Jeanne Lundell remembers dealing with three different developers and a bankruptcy or two. "We'd come to an agreement with one developer – we'll do this if you'll do this – then we'd have to go back to square one. When we finally began to see daylight at the end of the path, it was with a real sense of relief."[374]

In May 1989, the negotiations finally ended when the city accepted a 40-foot right-of-way and Lake Harbor agreed the setback would apply to an additional 30 feet.[375] Attempts in 1991 to push the bike path out into the streets of Lake Harbor were rejected.

Once Lake Harbor was in hand, the committee turned its attention to connecting it with the rest of the Greenbelt. The missing link was about a one-mile stretch from the Willow Lane Athletic Complex (a Greenbelt satellite park, also funded by the federal Land and Water Conservation Fund)[376] to Lake Harbor. This

---

372 LaMarche interview.
373 Kalbus interview.
374 Lundell interview.
375 Greenbelt Committee minutes, February 7, 1991
376 Cooper, "Capital Projects," pp. 3-4.

was more than a continuity issue. Without the Willow Lane-Lake Harbor link, people were forced to detour on city streets before they could get back on the Greenbelt. The job took nearly a decade, and for many committee members it ranks as their most satisfying achievement.

Joe LaMarche attributes the difficulty in making that connection to "some intervening residential ownerships that occurred along the riverbank. They had just enough clout to withstand the development of the pathway along the bank." There were six or eight homes along the edge of the river and one residence that was right on the riverbank.[377]

"In the very beginning it was economics," said Nancy Donald. The people who lived in the area wanted the absolute maximum payment for their houses, she said. "One time the Pioneer Title and the Ada County Realtors Association appraised the property as a donation. Even with that, it probably was 10 years later before we got anything done, which meant that (the appraisal) was a gift that was wasted."[378]

The Willow Lane/Heron Hollow area of the river was a very difficult area to survey. High water had created channels, which left some high spots that became islands during high-water years and others that were separated from the riverbank most of the year.[379] The meandering river also deposited new land in some areas and eroded property in others. As a result, to write accurate legal descriptions of the river and the floodplain was a complex and confusing task. After several years, and after much work by all concerned, the city obtained the Willow Lane land and the path was cleared. Ward Parkinson, a co-founder of Micron Technology who was active with the Boise River Trails Foundation, had a Trus Joist bridge installed so people could

---

377 LaMarche interview.
378 Donald interview.
379 Debowden Bauer, Boise City Parks & Recreation, written comments, emailed to author, April 4, 2001.

easily cross the islands. Once again, Donald said, the Greenbelt "really has added value to those people's neighborhood there."[380]

---

380 Donald interview.

8 Endings and Beginnings

"So I told them to start collecting money because we were coming through one way or the other."

– Judy Peavey-Derr on her plans to push the Greenbelt through Riverside Village

The long-running story of the Greenbelt pioneers does not end at Willow Lane. There are still miles to go.

During the decade of the 1990s, the Greenbelt Committee wrestled with intricate and sticky issues on both ends of the path. To the west it tried to find a way through the Plantation subdivision, which had been annexed by adjacent Garden City, a small, incorporated enclave surrounded on three sides by Boise. The committee also helped Garden City officials as they attempted to convince reluctant homeowners the Greenbelt should be allowed adjacent to Riverside Village, an upscale planned development in that city. Beyond Garden City, committee members and a new group, the Foundation for Ada-Canyon Trails System (FACTS), envisioned a path that stretched through to Eagle Island State Park, through Canyon County and on to the Snake River and the Oregon border, 50 miles west of Boise. To the east loomed Harris Ranch, a 1,710-acre mixed-use development and planned community near Barber Park, which at the time was preparing to sell lots.

To the credit of all concerned, the agreement between the city and Harris Ranch owners placed the Greenbelt along the river through the entire development and includes Marianne Williams Park.[381]

Boise city was also faced with the growing issue of safety along the Greenbelt. Two murders, in 1998 and 2000, and several assaults became tragic headlines and without question dimmed the glow of the city's pride in its No. 1 attraction.

But by 1997, Boise City decided the committee had done all it could. In November of that year, the Greenbelt Committee, under orders from the city, voted to disband. The park board absorbed its duties and two of its members.

W hen Judy Peavey-Derr was elected to the Ada County Commission in 1986, one of the issues that interested her the most was the opportunity to extend the Greenbelt through the unincorporated county. As part of the preparation for Idaho's state centennial in 1990, Eagle Mayor Steve Guerber proposed to connect the Greenbelt from Lucky Peak west all the way to the city of Eagle. Peavey-Derr loved the idea. At the same time, she knew Ada County government was not the appropriate mechanism to forge this link. Fellow commissioners Mike Johnson and Vern Bisterfelt were not as enthusiastic about the Greenbelt as she was, and it didn't take a crystal ball to see how the votes would go on the needed appropriations.

In 1987, Peavey-Derr created the Boise River Trail Foundation, a nonprofit 501(c)(3) organization, to extend the Greenbelt through Ada and Canyon counties. She asked Ward Parkinson, one of the founders

---

381   Bethann Stewart, "It's Been a Rocky Road for the Greenbelt," *Idaho Statesman*, March 15, 2008.

of Micron Technology and a Greenbelt supporter, to head it up. Peavey-Derr needed someone who could raise money. Parkinson knew how and who had it. She also knew that Parkinson owned 40 acres off Warm Springs Avenue on the Boise River and that he would be faced with the Greenbelt coming past his property some day. It took her almost two hours of conversation, but she convinced him. Parkinson became head of the Boise River Trail Foundation, which later became FACTS. The goal was to have a completely connected trail system from Lucky Peak Dam to Eagle Island State Park in three years.[382]

It was not a pipe dream. Peavey-Derr put her political skills to work and convinced representatives from the Idaho Transportation Department, Boise Parks & Recreation Department, the Greenbelt Committee, Boise's Ridge to Rivers trails coordinator, the Ada Planning Association, Ada County Parks, the Idaho Department of Parks and Recreation, Garden City Parks and Waterways, Idaho Department of Lands, Eagle Pathway and Parks, Eagle Island State Park, the cities of Caldwell, Kuna and Middleton, the Idaho State Garden Club and Canyon County to join her foundation.[383]

The first section the group finished was from Warm Springs Golf Club east to Eckert Road, along the abandoned Union Pacific right-of-way. Peavey-Derr had convinced Idaho Governor Cecil Andrus to find the $220,000 the foundation needed to purchase the old railroad property.

"Immediately, Parkinson paid for the engineering, Jim Nelson of Nelson Construction paid for the paving and the first mile was done," said Peavey-Derr. "We went out to see the newly paved path and found kids joy-riding, leaving big grooves in new asphalt."[384]

---

382 Judy Peavey-Derr interview with Troy Reeves, Boise, Idaho; August 4, 1998.
383 Lundell interview.
384 Peavey-Derr interview, Reeves.

Parkinson then challenged Boise Mayor Dirk Kempthorne to complete the path past the Warm Springs Golf Club and east toward the county's section of the path. Kempthorne was reluctant, but with good reason. The first issue was how to get a trail safely through a golf course. The second was that the course's private managers, who leased the course from the city, "were not enthralled with the concept," Jack Cooper said.

Eventually the city took advantage of the right-of-way abandoned by the Oregon Short Line Railroad and, after a long series of meetings and consultation with a golf course architectural firm, constructed large screens to protect Greenbelt users from golf balls and a careful alignment – which went off the river in places – that allowed both the course and the trail to work.[385] The county reciprocated on the west end when Commissioners Johnson and Bisterfelt agreed to pave the Ada County property behind what was then the Western Idaho Fairgrounds, now Expo Idaho, to Glenwood Street.

In 1989, the city linked the trail between Warm Springs Park and Municipal Park. With that task accomplished, the Greenbelt finally ran on the north side of the river from Lucky Peak State Park, west through Ann Morrison Park, to Veterans State Park and the Willow Lane Athletic Complex.

On the south side, however, for years the path stopped at Ann Morrison Park. That situation was corrected in 2015-2016 when the city constructed pathways and bridges to link the south side path from Ann Morrison Park to the Garden City path west of Main Street.

But farther west, the path ran into a new set of obstacles. Riverside Village is a planned subdivision of custom homes in Garden City located across Glenwood Street. It had built and paved its own path along the river's north bank, then closed it to the public and

---

385 Cooper, "Capital Expenditures," p. 2.

advertised, "the serenity of evening walks on a private greenbelt along the banks of the beautiful Boise River."[386]

When Peavey-Derr and the Garden City government attempted to extend the Boise Greenbelt across Glenwood to Riverside Village, she ran into "a firestorm" from some of the residents, she said. "They absolutely said no. 'You're not going to have the public behind us. We don't want the public through here.' They said they'd pay not to have it go behind them. So I told them to start collecting money because we were coming through one way or the other."

In response, Garden City began the long-term effort to buy two bridges upstream of Glenwood Street that would allow Greenbelt users to cross to the south side of the Boise River. The county then continued to push the path through along the river's south bank.[387]

Former Garden City Greenbelt Committee chair Christine Simon tells a different story. She remembers it was a group of Plantation homeowners, on the east side of Glenwood, who also didn't want the Greenbelt between them and the river. In 1990, in time for Idaho's centennial celebration, the Plantation homeowners put up $150,000 to pay for the two bridges Simon considers "shoddy," "inferior" and overpriced.[388]

Over the next several years, Garden City negotiated with Riverside Village to take over the private path and make it available to the public. During that time, the paved surface was invaded by cottonwood tree roots and became nearly impassible. The asphalt needed to be completely redone or removed, but Garden City's small budget had no such provision. Riverside Village homeowners, who still objected to having the path made public, said they would repair the path and turn it over only if it remained unpaved and no bicycles were allowed. Garden City agreed.

---

386 Stacy, *When the River Rises*, p. 103.
387 Peavey-Derr interview with the author, Boise, Idaho, May 29, 2001.
388 Christine Simon interview with the author; Boise, Idaho, Nov. 11, 2001.

This led to a path under Glenwood Street on the south side that continues all the way to the South Channel of the Boise River. The north side is accessible, though, by crossing at Glenwood Street or downstream at the Garden City West Bridge.

At the "No Trespassing" sign on the Garden City stretch of the path, in 1987. (Idaho Statesman Archives, BSU Special Collections)

The north side bike path runs for more than a mile through Riverside Village and Garden City streets, and eventually rejoins the river path at the entrance to Eagle's path.

Cyclists were not happy to be excluded from the Riverside Village portion of the path. A group called Citizens for an Open Greenbelt (COG) took the issue to the State Board of Land Commissioners in

2008 and argued the state's 1980 agreement with the subdivision's developer required a bike path. The commissioners disagreed.[389]

COG then raised $4,000 filing fees and other costs, and enlisted three attorneys who agreed to work *pro bono* to find a way to open the 1.5 mile path to bicycles and other non-motorized uses.[390]

In February 2012, 4th District Court dismissed COG's case and granted Garden City a summary judgment that allowed the city to restrict bicycle traffic on the pedestrian-only Riverside Nature Path.[391]

Garden City's response to the access issue was the long-sought bridge that would allow bicycle access to both sides of the river. The bridge installation began in May 2015. The $727,760 cost was paid by a federal grant.[392]

---

389 Bethann Stewart, "Garden City bike ban on Greenbelt OK," Idaho Statesman, October 11, 2008.

390 Nathaniel Hoffman, "COG IS BACK," *Boise Weekly*, May 5-11, 2010.

391 http://www.gardencityidaho.org/index.asp?SEC=B8DB513D-9135-48A9-BFD0-24345A0ACD15&Type=B BASIC

392 "Bridging the Pedestrian-Bike Divide," *Idaho Statesman*, May 2, 2015, p. A4.

Greenbelt advocate Judy Peavey-Derr.
(courtesy/Peavey-Derr)

"It isn't a perfect solution," said Peavey-Derr, "but it is the best compromise the community is going to get. It will be a wonderful biking experience and allow access to the river versus, going through communities and on busy streets the entire distance."[393]

When Peavey-Derr left county office in 1991, the drive to complete the county's portion of the Greenbelt left with her. She and Ward Parkinson tried to work with property owners, but without the "Commissioner" in front of her name, she no longer had the clout to get it done.

Not easily discouraged, Peavey-Derr changed the Boise River Trails Foundation to FACTS and for years held monthly meetings in an effort to keep the trail system moving toward Canyon County and ultimately to the Oregon border. FACTS fell short of its goal to reach Eagle Island by 2003, but the path now ends only a half mile from the state park.

Peavey-Derr said Parkinson and the committee "worked miracles but didn't get the path completed to (Eagle) Island in the time frame we were hoping. But they did get several sections done in break neck

393 Peavey-Derr, email to author, April 16, 2015.

speed. (Today a plaque and rest stop are located on the bike path near the Idaho Parks and Recreation Department Headquarters on Warm Springs Avenue near East Junior High commemorating the people on that committee and their efforts.)"[394]

Later, as an Ada County Highway District commissioner, again when she was as re-elected county commissioner, and then as trustee and board member of the Greater Boise Auditorium District, she continued her work with FACTS.

The section through Laguna Pointe in Eagle has proved to be another sticking point.

Eagle Mayor Nancy Merrill negotiated an easement with the first developer of Laguna Pointe, Peavey-Derr said. Unfortunately, she left office without recording the bike path easement. When the developer ran into financial trouble, the path fell by the wayside.

FACTS's effort to complete the bike path on the south side of the south channel all the way to Eagle Road was stopped by four Laguna Pointe homeowners.

"The developer had promised to build a parking lot for ten cars to use the bike path on his land next to Eagle Road," said Peavey-Derr. "That space is currently blocked off by boulders disallowing people from accessing the parking area. In my humble opinion this particular developer should have honored his verbal commitment as an honorable person....recorded or not...he didn't and the city of Eagle had to go to great expense to fix the problem."

The homeowners are still uncooperative and have placed a no loitering sign on a barbed wire fence along the path, she said.

The city of Eagle ordered the Laguna Pointe Homeowners Association to remove the barbed wire fence because it was unsafe for pedestrians and bicyclists who use the path. The fence remained in place. On April 21, 2015, the homeowners association sued the city

---

394 Peavey-Derr email.

because it delayed completion of the fence and caused the association to pay for hearing and appeal costs.

The association argued the barbed wire fence meets all federal requirements, the terms of a 2014 agreement with the city and deters trespassers. A wrought iron fence would cost $300,000, which could bankrupt the association, the lawsuit stated.[395]

"It's a work in progress," Scott Koberg, director of Ada County Parks and Waterways, said of the Greenbelt. "It's kind of getting stitched and pieced together, but we're gradually getting closer to Canyon County."[396]

In April 2004, the mayors of Boise and Garden City dedicated a section of the Greenbelt that linked the two cities on the south side of the Boise River: the paved path behind Joe's Crab Shack and the Doubletree Hotel Riverside (now the Riverside Hotel).[397]

Peavey-Derr has gone so far as to provide in her will for a portion of her estate to go to FACTS. "I am thoroughly convinced," she said, "that it's good for the air because as we get more people out and fewer people in cars; it's good for family relationships because it builds a bond; it's good for the health of any individual who chooses to walk or ride on the bike path; and I think it's good for the economy of the city because it is the crown jewel. Those four areas, to me, seem to be so important, that if I have in any way contributed to any one or all of them I feel my life goal has been very good."[398]

Harris Ranch was introduced to the Greenbelt Committee in October 1996. The plans called for the 1,710-acre ranch, located on the north side of the river east of Warm Springs

395 Katy Moeller, "HOA Sues Over Barbed Wire Fence, Parking," Idaho Statesman, May 1, 2015, p. A4.

396 Scott Koberg, interview with the author, April 16, 2015.

397 The Idaho Statesman, "New section of Greenbelt links Boise and Garden City," April 23, 2004.

398 Peavey-Derr interview, Reeves.

Golf Club and near Barber Park, to be developed into a planned community that would include both business and residential uses and 300 acres of open space.

An office full of issues had to be solved at Harris Ranch, including crucial access by way of the long-proposed East ParkCenter Bridge, which opened to traffic on September 29, 2009; the floodplain and floodway maps drawn by the Federal Emergency Management Agency; the alignment of State Highway 21; and the narrow access provided by Warm Springs Avenue as it squeezes between the Boise River and Warm Springs Mesa. But in Greenbelt terms, the matter was much simpler. The Harris Ranch owners wanted to put the pathway along Highway 21. The city wanted it along the river. In May 1997, the Greenbelt Committee recommended the path be along the river, and "in no case will the Greenbelt setback be less than 70 feet measured from the 6,500 cfs line of the Boise River."[399] "It's a river trail," said member Tom Baskin. "It always has been and that's what it was intended to be."[400]

"We spent hours and hours and hours with the developer at Harris Ranch, who was trying to keep it as far back from the river as possible," said Jeanne Lundell.[401]

"The connection of the Greenbelt through that project is a big deal," said Bob Whipkey. "In my estimation it would complete the path to the east."[402]

David Jones worried there would not be adequate parking in the new development. "The parking they proposed there seemed mainly to be contingent on the office development on the other side of the new West ParkCenter Bridge. It's the same problem as over in ParkCenter itself. What if the people who own those office buildings say, 'No, you're not going to be here'? The people of Boise deserve to

---

399 Greenbelt Committee minutes; May 7, 1997.
400 Tom Baskin interview with Troy Reeves, Boise, Idaho; July 16, 1998
401 Lundell interview.
402 Whipkey interview.

have access to the Greenbelt, and we need to do our best to make sure they have it and that it's not a situation where they have to get up at 8:00 in the morning to get a parking spot."[403]

Wayne Gibbs felt public pressure would be the city's ace in the hole, what would force Harris Ranch to locate the path near the river. But he and Peter O'Neill agree that it is unfortunate the city didn't start the process years ago.

"If we had gotten our act together before Harris Ranch was an issue, maybe we could have acquired some of that land," Gibbs said.[404]

"My argument, way back before it was ever planned, was, 'Let's work with the property owners and make a decision today about what should happen there so it doesn't get subjected to this insanity we go through,'" said O'Neill.[405]

---

403 Jones interview.
404 Gibbs interview.
405 O'Neill interview.

*Earl Reynolds (center) with his wife Harriett and then-Mayor Dirk
Kempthorne (1986-92). Reynolds was a volunteer in city activities, on
planning and zoning, the Greenbelt Committee and the city parks
board for 30 years. (Idaho Statesman Archives, BSU Special
Collections)*

hile Boise has long prided itself as a family-oriented
town, a safe place to live and work, it is not Brigadoon or
Camelot. The history of the Greenbelt includes the
murders of Kay Lynn Jackson in 1998 and Lynn Henneman in
September 2000, plus an uncounted number of reported and
unreported major and minor assaults over the years. A survey of 1,300
residents in January and February 2001 showed almost half of the
respondents were at least moderately concerned about their safety
while on the Greenbelt.[406]

The city responded by creating the Greenbelt Safety Patrol, a
combination of trained volunteers in motorized golf carts and
mounted and bicycle police officers. It also cut growth away from the
trail, put lights in tunnels and fenced areas around overpasses to
eliminate potential hiding places.

These efforts paid off. In response to the 2012 survey conducted by
Boise State University's Department of Community and Regional
Planning of 1,224 Greenbelt users, 90 percent said they felt safe. In
the survey's comments section, 212 respondents wrote "Love it,"
another 83 respondents said the Greenbelt was "Great for Boise," 30
wrote "Thanks" and 13 wrote "I enjoy it."[407]

The 2013 and 2014 surveys echoed these sentiments.

In the volunteer spirit of the Greenbelt pioneers, Eagle Scout Josh
Taylor and high school student Jennifer Sayer took up the cause of
safety themselves and put forth two separate proposals.

In 2001, Taylor planned and created the Distance and Orientation
Trail System. DOTS is a point-of-reference system that locates the

---

406   Wayne Hoffman, "Ada Residents Still Worry About Greenbelt Safety," *Idaho Statesman,*
April 26, 2001, p.1.

407   greenbelt_report-1.pdf ps://parks.cityofboise.org/media/947246/Urban-Research_May-
2014_final.pdf, p.7

user anywhere along the path. Taylor and his volunteers painted a series of 20-inch white dots every tenth of a mile along the Greenbelt near and within Boise city. Inside the 112 dots are black numbers and letters that correspond with their distance from the Capitol Boulevard bridge and the side of the river on which the DOT is located. The designation NE 3.1 means the person is on the north side of the river and 3.1 miles east of 8th Street pedestrian bridge. SW 0.8 is located on the south side of the river, 0.8 miles west of 8th Street.[408]

Sayer's goal was to have the city install lights along the Greenbelt. Her research revealed that each 20-foot light would cost about $500. She took the results of her work to the city and asked the city to install 10 lights per year.[409]

In August 2001, a group that called itself the Citizens' Committee for Greenbelt Safety proposed Boise light the path along the 2.5 miles from Kathryn Albertson Park to Municipal Park at a cost of $187,000.[410]

On October 16, 2001, the Boise City Council approved $187, 620 "to install greenbelt lighting from Main Street Bridge to Municipal Park on both sides of the Boise River" as part of its 2002-2003 budget capital expenditures.[411]

---

408 http://parks.cityofboise.org/parks-locations/parks/greenbelt/

409 Wayne Hoffman, "Can't Fight City Hall? Don't Tell That to Jennifer Sayer," *The Idaho Statesman,* June 9, 2001, p.1.

410 Greenbelt Committee minutes, Sept. 16 1997.

411 Boise City Council minutes, Oct. 16, 2001, www.ci.boise.id.us/city_clerk/minutes/101601m.pdf

The city held the ceremonial last meeting of Boise Greenbelt and Pathways Committee in the elegantly refurbished Boise Depot, November 3, 1997, with a business meeting and a proclamation by Mayor Brent Coles.

The first public notice the committee might be on its way out had come only about two weeks earlier, September 16, 1997, when the committee addressed the possibility that its duties might be merged into those of the park board. A motion was approved to recommend "the Board of Park and Recreation Commissioners by motion dissolve the Greenbelt and Pathways Committee effective November 1, 1997, and assume the responsibilities of that body relative to the Boise River System Ordinance."[412]

"A consensus developed that our services were no longer needed," said Tom Baskin.[413] Baskin and Greenbelt pioneer Earl Reynolds became members of the newly reorganized and enlarged parks board.

Mayor H. Brent Coles, 1992-2003. (Boise City Department of Arts & History)

The action prompted a wide variety of reactions. Some Greenbelt members, such as Dede Wilhelm, felt it was redundant to have two

412 Greenbelt Committee minutes, Sept. 16. 1997.
413 Baskin interview.

groups, the committee and the parks board, work on the same issues at the latter stages of the Greenbelt's expansion.[414]

Earl Reynolds felt the old system wasn't working anymore. He could do more good, he thought, from his new seat on the park board. When he joined the Greenbelt Committee the city's population was 34,000. In 1997, at 150,000-plus, the issues were bigger and needed more specialized attention. "I think the present organization is better fitted for the 21st century," he said.[415]

Joe LaMarche worried the park board would have too much on its plate to pay proper attention to the Greenbelt, that pressure to create new parks and ball diamonds will leave the pathway overlooked. "I think it's up to the general public and the parks department itself to recognize the responsibility and watch out for the Greenbelt," he said.[416]

Another point of view came from those who were frustrated after long years of being limited to advisory status. Some believed the committee's status within city government had declined over several years, leaving it a powerless remnant of what it was 30 years before.

"We felt like, and we had for about 10 years, that we had no power, that we were under the jurisdiction of Boise Parks Department, and it was rather futile," said Nancy Donald, who described the committee as the stepchild of the parks department. "We'd spend hours and hours reviewing a project and making a decision about it, and the parks department had the authority and power to change whatever we said. Then we were directed by (Parks director) Jim Hall to disband. But we all felt what we'd done was valuable and worthwhile."[417]

---

414 Wilhelm interview.
415 Reynolds interview.
416 LaMarche interview.
417 Donald interview.

Jim Hall, 2012. Boise Parks & Recreation Director. (Boise Parks & Recreation Department)

Jim Kalbus, Robert Stolz, Bert Cleaveland and Joe LaMarche also characterized the committee's advisory status as "frustrating." It was hard not to have any enforcement power, said Kalbus,[418] and Stolz described having seemingly every decision go from the committee to the park board, to the parks department, to the city council and the mayor. "It was a less-than-efficient method to get your way," he said.[419]

"It should have been a separate committee that answered to the city council," said Mike Misner.[420] Joe LaMarche lobbied unsuccessfully for the committee to have its own budget.[421]

"At times, we would send our recommendations to the park board, and they wouldn't pass them on," said Jeanne Lundell. "It felt like they disregarded the study and the time we put into it. It really created some problems."[422]

But as Earl Reynolds saw it, "We can't all be king. There are a lot of other people out there with opinions." Still, he found it frustrating when he came back on the Greenbelt Committee and found it had

---

418 Kalbus interview.
419 Robert Stolz interview.
420 Mike Misner interview.
421 LaMarche interview.
422 Lundell interview

been absorbed by the park board. "On the park board there just weren't the advocates for the Greenbelt who had no other interests when the final decisions were made." Reynolds hoped the new pathways subcommittee of the parks board would act as a strong voice for the Greenbelt.[423]

Susan Stacy, though she never served on the committee, regrets its demise. "I think it might have disbanded too soon, because they were tremendous advocates. They were single-minded and had a single purpose, which you don't find on a larger board," she said.[424]

By all rights, the Greenbelt should never have happened. Everything was lined up against it. It was 10 years too late. The city was going through a costly downtown redevelopment and had a myopic fixation on the creation of a downtown mall. Then came the One Percent Initiative. The economy went into the tank. Many Idahoans did and still do feel strongly about private property rights. Developers such as Morrison Knudsen Corp. were the powers behind the thrones. The city had no money to spend on it, and the Greenbelt Committee had advisory power only. But the Greenbelt did happen. Thanks to the courage, vision and work ethic of a handful of self-sacrificing civic pioneers, for what in retrospect was almost no money, the city acquired what has become a nearly priceless asset.

Earl Reynolds credited it to a symbiotic/synergistic relationship between the Greenbelt and the people. The more people got involved in the project, the better it looked and the more supporters it attracted. Reynolds was too modest. That energy, that willingness to overcome an entire city's natural inertia, had to start somewhere. That somewhere was with a small group of courageous Boise residents who got caught up in an idea; an idea they thought could benefit the

---

423 Reynolds interview.
424 Stacy interview.

community and everyone in it for decades to come, and they were willing to invest enormous amounts of time and energy to make the idea into something real. That belief then spread to the community at large. That is why Boise has the Greenbelt today.

It was not like the successful Foothills levy of 2001 and the Open Space levy of 2015, in which Boiseans, in a startling reversal of their historic voting patterns, agreed to raise their own property taxes temporarily to buy and preserve Foothills land. It wasn't the city government or city taxes that made the Greenbelt happen. It was a few believers who had the dream, then joined the government to make it happen. It was grass-roots activism in the best possible sense.

They were people willing to act, to take a chance that things would work out even if they weren't quite sure how. What if the Greenbelt pioneers had been cautious types? What if they had waited to do it perfectly, had waited until they had the money and the property lined up and everyone on board before they began the campaign? The answer is simple: The Greenbelt we know today would not exist. And neither would the city of Boise.

"There will always be people who say we haven't done enough or that we've done too much," said former city council member Mike Wetherell. "But given the limited fund base Idaho cities have, I'd say we've done a fine job preserving our riverfront for public use."[425]

Unfortunately, the Idaho Legislature has made it much more difficult for any government entity to duplicate Boise's remarkable story.

The 2015 Legislature passed SB1044, which barred local governments from using the power of eminent domain to obtain land "for trails, paths, greenways or other ways for walking, running, hiking, bicycling or equestrian use, unless adjacent to a highway, road

---

425 Candice Chung, "The Greenbelt Still Is a Path in Progress," *Idaho Statesman*, July 7, 1997, p. 1A.

or street."[426] It was nothing less than an anti-greenbelt law, passed despite the easily demonstrated success and overwhelming popularity of Boise's effort.

Judy Peavey-Derr described the new law as "short sighted" and "terribly unfortunate." She added, "It addressed a problem that didn't exist by the state delving into local politics. It will affect safe routes to school for school children, and it will impede economic development not to mention transportation via bikes to work.

"Bike paths are a wonderful amenity to any community.....just look at Weiser, and northern Idaho. We need these tools in our rural communities to attract tourism and therefore economic development."[427]

Forty-five years after the idea was launched, much of the dust has settled. Most of the arguments have been made, most of the legal action concluded. The Boise City portion of the Boise River Greenbelt is complete and the dream of taking it to the Oregon border survives.

So, who won in the battles over property and access rights, the clashes between egos, the turf wars, the funding problems and the genuine, principled disagreements over methods and philosophy?

It's not a difficult question to answer.

Go down to the Boise Greenbelt any time of year. See the remarkable variety of ways in which people propel themselves through this linear system of parks and open space. Watch the walkers, runners, rollerbladers, bikers and tubers. Go during the warm weather and see the picnickers, anglers, waders, sleepers and river floaters. Play a little yourself. Fly a kite or a Frisbee. See the ducks. Watch soccer and softball in the parks. Feel the temperature drop as you find the shade near the river. Inhale. Enjoy.

You won. Boise won. We all won.

---

426 http://www.legislature.idaho.gov/legislation/2015/S1044.htm
427 Peavey-Derr, email, April 16, 2015.

At the 2016 construction around Broadway Bridge. (David Proctor)

Acknowledgements

This book had a long gestation period, and there were many people who helped it see the light of day.

Most important, my deep thanks to the Greenbelt pioneers. We all owe them more than we can ever repay.

Thanks also to Troy Reeves, who did the original Greenbelt pioneer interviews, and to Susan Stacy, whose book *When the River Rises: Flood Control on the Boise River 1943-1985*, was of invaluable assistance on this project.

I'm also very grateful for the assistance offered by Kathleen Barrett, Boise Parks & Recreation Department (retired); Sarah Collings, Boise Parks & Recreation Department; Scott Koberg, Ada County Parks and Waterways; Cheryl Oestreicher and Jim Duran of the Special Collections and Archives in the Albertson Library at Boise State University; Terry Schorzman, director, Brandi Burns, history programs manager, and the rest of the staff of the Boise Arts & History Department; to Mayor David Bieter for his generous introduction and to Randy Stapilus and Linda Watkins at Ridenbaugh Press for their editorial talents and patience.

Finally, great thanks and much love to my wife, Becky, for her unfailing support.

Index

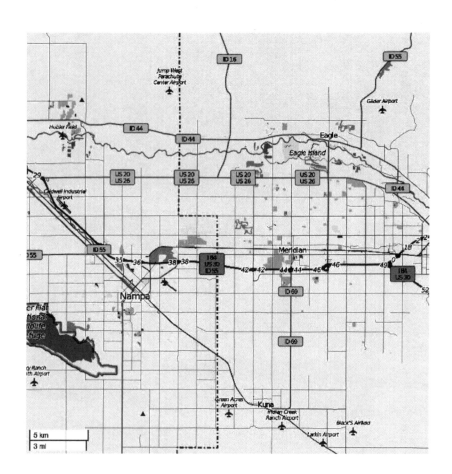

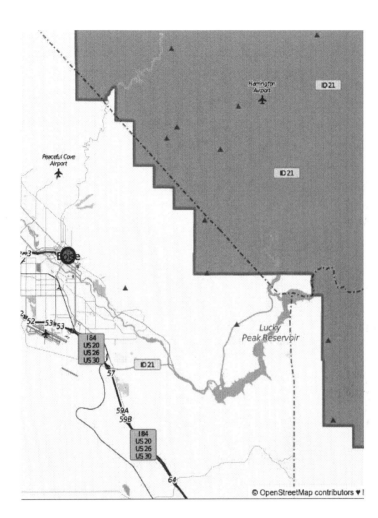

David Proctor is an award-winning journalist and author who has lived in Vermont, Maryland (twice), Germany (twice), Kentucky, Indiana, Utah and Idaho. He has a master's degree in communications/journalism from the University of Utah, and his work has appeared in *The Salt Lake Tribune*, *The Daily Utah Chronicle*, *Utah Holiday* magazine, *Rolling Stone*, *The Great Salt Lake Newspaper*, *Zoo World*, the *Idaho Mountain Express*, the *Idaho Statesman*, *USA Today*, and on Gannett News Service and Reuters. He also founded and directed the Log Cabin BookFest, and was the award-winning director of media and public relations for The Idaho Foodbank.

His previous books include *The Quotable Vampire* and *My Oregon Life* (with Elvine Gienger) and *Brothers Alpha*, all available on Amazon. He is a member of the Boise City Ethics Commission and a volunteer instructor with Boise Community Education. He lives in Boise, Idaho, with his family.

He is the father of two grown daughters and has been married to Becky for 35 years.

Made in the USA
San Bernardino, CA
06 July 2016